BASIC BOOK OF **CLOCHE & FRAME GARDENING**

BASIC BOOK OF
CLOCHE &
FRAME GARDENING

W. E. SHEWELL-COOPER
MBE, NDH, FLS, FRSL, MRST, Dip.Hort.(Wye), DLitt

BARRIE & JENKINS
COMMUNICA-EUROPA

First published in 1977
by Barrie & Jenkins Ltd
24 Highbury Crescent, London N5 1RX

ISBN 0 214 20301 8

Printed in Great Britain
by W & J Mackay Limited, Chatham
by photo-litho

Phototypeset in Great Britain by
Filmtype Services Limited, Scarborough

Contents

List of illustrations

Acknowledgements

The author would like to thank Imperial Chemical Industries Ltd, Plant Protection Division for the black-and-white photograph on page 15, and Access-Crick Ltd for those on pages 20, 21, 22, 47, 66, 79, 90, 93, 109, 129, 134 and 142.

Preface

Cloches and frames are an excellent means to achieve greater, earlier, faster or out-of-season production than by uncovered planting in open ground. The effect is just like that of a greenhouse, with the difference that you take the greenhouse to the plants rather than the plants to the greenhouse. Cloches and frames are, of course, much cheaper than greenhouses, and are ideal for those who only want to grow a few plants at any one time.

For another reason, they are very useful if you want large and continuous crops. Because these glass or plastic structures warm the soil beneath them, plants develop much more quickly and you can therefore put a piece of ground to optimum use by planting, say, two or three crops a season instead of one. By heating the ground electrically, the process is speeded up even more, and cloches and frames can be most valuable in the winter months too.

I can recommend cloches and frames to all gardeners, whatever the size of their garden, who have never tried them.

W. E. SHEWELL-COOPER

Arkley Manor,
Arkley,
South Herts.

1 Introduction to cloches and frames

The word 'cloche' is French for a bell. A long time ago French market gardeners evolved a glass jar in the shape of a bell, which they used for speeding the growth of their plants. These cloches had no automatic ventilation. In the early years of this century a continuous cloche was devised and patented; this was an entirely new concept, as it provided glass protection for whole rows of plants. The advantage of continuous cloches is that they can provide almost automatic ventilation and yet give all the protection required.

Bell jars or cloches in a market garden in Croisy near Paris

In Britain the gardener's chief winter enemy is damp – plants suffer far more from damp than they do from frost. Rock gardeners have known this for a long time, and protect their plants in the winter by covering them with a sheet of glass held a few inches above them. Cloches are of great value in the winter, for not only do they keep out the wet, but several degrees of frost too. They give ideal protection from wind, not only from the icy blasts of winter but also from drying summer winds. The ends of the cloche rows should always be kept closed, to prevent them from becoming wind tunnels.

Cloches and frames are a necessity and not an extra. They are just as much used by the market gardener as they are by the home grower. They are equally excellent in thousands, covering a large area, or in their dozens or less on an allotment or in an average-sized garden.

At one time they were used almost entirely for vegetables, but today they are popular for flowers too – annuals, perennials and bulbs. It was also thought they had no use in the summer, but now they are used with great success to grow melons and cucumbers, to ripen off onions and shallots, and for taking cuttings of herbaceous flowers and shrubs.

Cloches are not cumbersome to move about from place to place and the minimum of time and labour is used if the strip system (see page 37) is adopted.

Types of cloche
There are three main types of cloches – the tent, the barn and the various plastic ones.

1, TENT CLOCHE   This consists of two sheets of glass held firmly in position by a patented wiring system consisting of a base wire and a handle. This holds the cloches perfectly rigid, and yet the shade produced by the wires is negligible. The handle allows the cloche to be ventilated by sliding one sheet of glass into the notches. This gives a space about 1 in. wide right along the ridge of the cloche, too small to let in birds or any appreciable amount of rain, but wide enough to keep the inside of the cloche reasonably cool, even in the hottest weather.

A tent cloche

2. BARN CLOCHE   This consists of four sheets of glass held together by four wires, a handle (interchangeable with that used in the tent cloche), a base wire, an eaves wire and a panel. The barn type is also perfectly rigid and one can easily be carried in each hand. Ventilation is provided along the ridge in just the same way as in the tent pattern.

The panel allows a roof glass to be removed entirely, making it unnessary to move the cloche when working on the plants beneath. The cloche still remain rigid because the panel is designed to act as a compression member when the roof glass is removed. The whole thing is a quick and simple operation.

You can imagine what a difference the panel makes when growing a crop of frame cucumbers or melons, where the plants have to be stopped and, in the case of melons, the flowers have to be pollinated. Without it, each cloche in the row would have to be moved and put back carefully in exactly the right position. With the panel, cloches need never be moved, except from crop to crop. Think what this means in the winter, when violets or polyanthus have to be picked from under the cloches! Sometimes cloches get frozen to the ground and it is impossible to lift them – but it is possible to pick flowers from beneath barn cloches whatever the conditions.

A barn cloche

Until the ventilating handle was introduced, the usual procedure when extra ventilation was required was to space the cloches out so that they stood a few inches apart. This was quite effective, though laborious, but it had one or two disadvantages. In the first place, if the space was too wide birds could get in. In the second place, the ventilation was from top to bottom, whereas horticulturally it is far better to have it come through the roof. The other method of giving extra ventilation, i.e.

removing the ends of the rows, is not at all advisable because it causes dangerous draughts. The ventilating handle enables top ventilation to be given to each cloche. The glass slides easily into the ventilating notch, and the cloche remains perfectly rigid.

It is not necessary to open and close the cloches every day. In a hot spell all the cloches can be given top ventilation, or, if preferred, every third or fourth cloche, just as in a greenhouse one opens ventilators at intervals along the top of the roof. The job is simple, quick and effective. As a rule most crops do better with a small amount of top ventilation from May onwards, except in cold districts or during cold weather. Tent and barn cloches can both be ventilated in this way.

The cloches are very simple to assemble, and can be erected or taken to pieces in a few seconds. As a matter of fact it is seldom necessary to take them to pieces once they have been put together, for the keen gardener will find a use for them all the year round, and directly they are taken off one row of plants they will go over another.

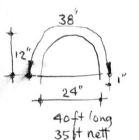

3. POLYTHENE TUNNEL CLOCHE Instead of individual cloches standing as close together as possible, this type forms a complete tunnel from a sheet of 150 gauge polythene, 40 ft long and 40 in. wide. The tunnel is erected on 11 supporting carved hoops, and has 11 securing wires. This will make up a 35-ft length of continuous cloche, or two 15-ft cloches, or three 10-ft cloches. Once erected, secure the tunnel well so that the polythene sheet does not blow away. It is easy to lift the sides of the tunnel for weeding, hoeing or harvesting.

These long, low cloches can be used for growing crops like lettuce, spinach, radishes, turnips, beetroot, beans and carrots. Strawberries crop very early under this type. If you lift up the edge of the cloche on the lee side during the flowering period, and then close it down in the evening, pollination is assured. Be prepared to water well in a dry season.

The polythene sheet should last for two seasons if it is stored out of sunlight in midsummer when it is not in use.

4. NOVOLUX CLOCHE These plastic cloches are made of lightweight, rigid PVC; they are curved and give a cloche length of either 3 ft or 6 ft.

The 3-ft cloche consists of a tough, transparent, corrugated vinyl sheet, which is bent into an arc and fitted into two strong galvanized frames, whose legs penetrate the ground to a depth

A polythene tunnel cloche

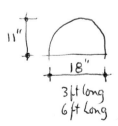

of 7½ in. The two end pieces are flat vinyl sheets, held firmly in position with canes (not supplied).

The 6-ft cloche consists of two corrugated vinyl sheets (which can be overlapped when joined), four galvanized frames and two end pieces. The width is 18 in. and the height 11 in.

Each individual cloche can be made up as a small, complete unit, but the length can be increased by joining together two or more cloches, either overlapping the ends slightly or butt-joining them for extra ventilation.

In very exposed situations the cloches can be further secured against strong winds by passing a cord through the frame loops

A Novolux cloche

and tying the ends to short stakes placed in the ground about 18 in. from the ends of the cloches.

These cloches, like the glass types, can be used all the year round, and crops are grown in the same way. Place them in position about a week before sowing to allow the ground to warm up; keep the end pieces in position at all times to prevent the cloche becoming a wind tunnel.

The advantages of PVC cloches, of course, are that they do not break and are quite rigid. They are just as transparent as ordinary glass, and on the whole let in more infra-red light.

They can put up with a good deal of ill treatment from animals and children. They are, of course, rotproof, and the galvanized wires that keep them in position last well.

5. ROBINSON'S 'SUPER' CLOCHE   These cloches are made from Dulite Corrox, a revolutionary new type of polypropylene sheeting. Two layers of film are held apart by internal webbing, giving a box-like section structure with built-in air space. The cloche allows good light penetration, refracting it in all directions to produce gentle, diffused light throughout the day. The thermal non-conductivity is about eight times that of traditional material, and the double layer virtually eliminates condensation.

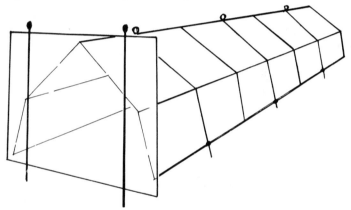

Robinson's 'Super' cloche, with an end panel in position

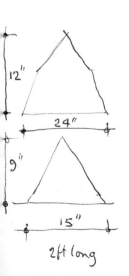

The Dulite cover is 4 mm thick and virtually unbreakable; its life is probably about five years if the cloches are constantly exposed. The material is unaffected by frost. Each cloche is held perfectly still under a heavy-duty galvanized wire hoop. The cover is held firmly by tight rubber grummets at the base of each side. The wires extend right into the ground to ensure firm anchorage. Panels are provided for closing the ends of the cloche rows.

There are two types: (a) the barn, which is 24 in. long × 12 in. high × 24 in. wide, and (b) the tent, which is 24 in. long × 9 in. high × 15 in. wide.

The simple frame or dutch light
Originally, frames were completely built with brick walls, the wall at the back 6 in. or so higher than the wall in the ground,

12 -13 .
19 - 21
24 - 27

and the side walls sloping, to accommodate the two different levels. The frame lights consisted of a strong framework with two bars holding narrow panes of glass, say 9 × 12 in., which invariably overlapped. The overlap used to fill up with green algae, and too much shade was produced. The lights were generally heavy and cumbersome.

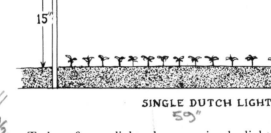

15″   12″
4″

SINGLE DUTCH LIGHT
59″

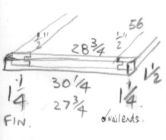

56
28¾   ½″   ½″   1½
½″
¼   30¼   ¼   1¼
¼   27¾   ¼
FIN.   ∂nailends.

Today, frame lights have a simple lightweight wooden framework. The sides of this framework are grooved to take a single sheet of 24-oz glass 56 × 28¾ in. This large pane of glass is held firmly in position by wooden stops which are firmly nailed to the end of the frame. This framework plus glass is known as a dutch light.

These dutch lights are placed on a framework of boards 15 in. wide at the back and only 9 in. wide in front. The length of the frame is 59 in. and its width is 30¼ in. Very often the frames consist of three dutch lights placed on the prepared open-shaped bottomless box, side by side.

These frames give protection against at least 8 degrees of frost and against the damage that is invariably done by high winds and excessive rain. You can introduce soil warming units into the frames, with the result that crops grow even faster.

The ideal unit for a family of four is probably two wooden frames, each of them holding three dutch lights, placed straight on the ground. The wooden frames should be light enough to move from place to place as needed. It pays to treat the wood with Rentokil preservative – don't use tar or creosote because they will kill the plants. I have known frames treated with Rentokil to last 20 years.

The soil on which the frame is seated must be rich in organic matter. Fork in compost at 2 large bucketsful to the square yard. If you haven't made compost, use sedge peat plus a good fish manure at 4 oz. to the square yard. The frame and the lights must be in position for about a fortnight before sowing the seeds and putting out the plants, so as to warm up the soil. It is, however, not only warmth that the roots of plants need but moisture as well. So the soil used in the frames must hold enough water. To water heavily in the spring and autumn cools down the soil and does harm to the roots. The addition of plenty of organic matter ensures that the moisture given in the winter is held until needed by the plants. In the summer, water may be given liberally from a sprinkler. This is best given early in the morning, so that the foliage will be dry by nightfall.

The choice of the site for the frames is important : (a) it should be in a spot sheltered from north and east winds, (b) it should be where the frames can get the maximum unobstructed light and (c) never select a low lying spot where frozen air may collect.

Unlike continuous cloches, frames have no natural automatic ventilation. Dutch lights must be raised on to a small wooden block, $6 \times 3 \times 2$ in. When a little ventilation is required, lay the block on its side; if more ventilation is needed, stand the block on its end. Always ventilate, as it were, on the lee side, and never have winds blowing directly into the frame.

The general rules about ventilating a frame are (1) don't admit air when the seeds are germinating; (2) don't give air to a newly-planted crop until it has obviously established itself; (3) close the frames when the sun starts to go down; (4) in the winter open the frames a little at the bottom only; (5) if there has been a sharp frost overnight, ventilate carefully by opening the dutch light slightly so that a little air is provided before the sunshine reaches the glass to cause a sudden thaw – it is this *sudden* thawing out that causes damage to some plants; and (6) never open the lights wide when rain could drive in, when there is fog or when there is serious frost.

Weeds must be kept down in the frame, so that they do not compete with the crops. Use a small hand hoe or weed by hand. You can prevent annual weeds from growing by covering the soil, after planting, with sedge peat ½ in. deep. This is expensive but the plants appreciate it and so will you if it minimizes your weeding.

If winds are a nuisance in the garden, tie down the lights by driving in large nails on either side of the wooden frame. Then stretch a cord or length of telephone wire tightly from one nail to the other. If serious frosts are likely, cover the glass light with a strip of sacking or a length of old blanket.

In midsummer when it is very sunny it is advisable to apply

some whitewash to the outside of the glass; this prevents scorch, especially on melons and cucumbers. Never apply whitewash when growing tomatoes or lettuces, however.

Access frames

To put it simply, the Access frame is a kind of rigid, elongated cloche. It is, in fact, far more like a large barn cloche than a dutch light on a wooden box frame.

An Access frame

The 10 × 4 is, in fact, a large-capacity, straight up and down, well-constructed frame or cloche; it has vertical sides and no waste space. The pressure-treated built-in base can stand with confidence on the soil.

Mist irrigation, i.e. spraying the plants constantly with mist, can be introduced into the frames, and this is a great time-saver. The frames are attractive and have a long, maintenance-free life. They can be opened up for ventilation by sliding the side or top panes (finger grips are provided).

The panels of glass are held safely in channels, and there is no puttying. The edges of the panes can be made safe by using a safe-edge pad to smoothe any roughness. The metal part of this elongated cloche is galvanized, and is easily put together and dismantled with wing nuts and bolts.

Access frames can be heated with an Access portable fan

heater. This is thermostatically controlled, and gives a good distribution of heat right down the length of the frame. It is possible to keep out 6 to 7 degrees of frost. Soil-warming cables can also be used with success.

A mist line irrigating an Access frame

The Access frame has been designed to be moved from site to site, so that one crop can be brought on to maturity and then the frame moved on to another crop.

As with all cloches, organic matter in the soil is absolutely essential to get the most out of the frame. Well-prepared compost or sedge peat should be forked into the ground in the autumn at the rate of 1 large bucketful to the yard run. Fish manure, hoof and horn, or any other organic compound fertilizer should be added at about 3 oz to the square yard. Before sowing or planting, however, do make sure that the soil is moist enough – the Access mist line is ideal for watering the soil adequately. As with cloches, put the frame in position 7–10 days before sowing seeds or putting in plants, in order to warm up the soil.

Regular watering is important, as plants are almost 95 per cent water. Once again, the Access overhead mist line is ideal for this purpose. Foliage feeding can be carried out during the summer with a seaweed liquid manure, which also helps to control pests and diseases.

Ventilation is simple. In the spring open the corner sheets on each side of the frame 1–3 in. As the weather gets warmer, give top ventilation by sliding the glass panels open. If the plants themselves are adequately watered, they can, curiously enough, stand quite high temperatures. Shading is therefore rarely required. Clean the glass every autumn. In the summer the top panes of glass can be removed altogether – the bottom panels give wind protection and yet all plants can grow out of the frame.

Provided the soil is properly fed with compost and enough water is given, cropping can be very intensive. It is usually advisable to plant one crop between two rows of another crop. Lettuces, for instance, do well between beans, peas or carrots. In one corner of the Access frame a square of parsley can be sown, or a short row of radishes can be included. With proper planning, in fact, every square inch of frame can be put to work effectively.

Intensive cropping under an Access frame

2 Soil preparation

Experiments carried out at Rothamsted Experimental Station show that deep cultivation is by no means as necessary as gardeners used to think. Soil to be covered with cloches or frames only needs to be cultivated to a depth of 2–3 in.

Soil

FORKING A fork will enable you to get the surface soil down to a fine tilth. It is impossible to produce this tilth if the soil is sticky and wet, which is where cloches and frames play their part. They may be put into position a week or fortnight before the seed is to be sown, and will not only dry out the soil, but warm it up as well. This makes the fine tilth necessary for seed sowing very easily produced.

TREADING AND RAKING These are often done to break up the clods. In stony soils there is no need to try to rake away every single stone that appears. In fact a few stones are useful, for they help to keep the soil moist underneath.

HOEING For some reason or other, many amateur gardeners hate hoeing more than anything else. By using cloches and frames, hoeing is reduced to a minimum. The glass or plastic covers seem to provide their own dust mulch on the surface of the soil; this prevents moisture for evaporating, and keeps it down below where the plant roots need it. From time to time raking or hoeing under the cloches or frames may be necessary – use short hoes and rakes for this.

LIME It is most important that soils should not be acid. Lime sweetens the soil and improves the texture and workability of clays. It adds calcium as a plant food, and because it helps to decompose humus and organic compounds it releases other plant foods. Because of this, when continuous cloches are used, more crops per annum can be obtained.

Lime should always be applied on the surface of the ground after other manures have been forked in. It is not so important for potatoes and roots as it is for peas, beans and cabbage. Hydrated lime is the simplest to use, and the normal application is 3, 4 or 5 oz to the square yard, according to the acidity.

ANALYSING SOIL FOR ACIDITY OR ALKALINITY   Acidity and alkalinity in soil are denoted by numbers on the pH scale: pH 7 represents the neutral point; figures less than 7 indicate increasing degrees of acidity, and figures above 7 increasing degrees of alkalinity.

The extremes of soil acidity and alkalinity in Britain usually vary between pH 8·5 and 4·5, and most crops do best in soils which range from pH 6 to 7·5. Of course, different crops prefer different soil conditions – for instance, peas and beans seem to like a soil between pH 6 and 7, but potatoes prefer a soil from pH 4·7 to 5·7. A simple soil-testing kit, complete with instructions, can be bought from chemists and garden shops.

Manure and fertilizers

It is most important, when growing plants under cloches and frames, to see that the soil is enriched with plenty of organic matter; old animal manure or browny-black powdery compost should be buried 5–6 in. down at the rate of one 2-gallon bucketful to a square yard. If old dung is not available, composted seaweed or specially composted vegetable refuse may be used (see below). Make sure that there is a good layer of well-rotted organic matter incorporated in the top 4 in. or so. It is a good plan to soak the bottom of the shallow trench thoroughly when digging.

It is also advisable, when using cloches, to rake in to the top soil, powdery damped sedge peat or, if preferred, dark brown compost. This gives the little seedlings a good start until they can send their roots down to the organic manure below. The peat or compost should be used at a 2-gallon bucketful to the square yard.

The flavour and food value of vegetables cannot be kept at a high level if the soil is not enriched with organic matter each year. This not only assists in the aeration of the soil and helps to produce a better mechanical and physical condition, but also provides humus, which is very important. Organic manures are also valuable for the way in which they help to liberate plant foods already present in the soil.

ORGANIC FERTILIZERS   It will also be necessary to add organic fertilizers with a fish or meat and bone base. Use 3–4 oz to the square yard, and apply them to the surface of the ground. They can easily be worked in with a rake.

Hoof and horn meal is another slow-acting manure which contains nitrogen and phosphates plus the necessary organic matter. Use this at 4 oz to the square yard together with, say, wood ashes at 8 oz to the square yard.

Soot helps to darken light soils, which enables them to absorb and retain heat better. It should be used principally for members of the cabbage family in the spring, at the rate of 5 oz to the square yard.

CHEMICAL FERTILIZERS In addition to fertilizers with an organic base, it may be necessary to apply some extra potash, particularly on light soils, and sulphate of potash may be applied at 1 oz to the square yard during seed bed preparation. Alternatively use wood ashes at about ½ lb to the square yard.

COMPOSTING VEGETABLE REFUSE A very good substitute for dung can be made with vegetable refuse from the house, garden or allotment. The Horticultural Training College at Arkley recommends a method of composting which avoids having to turn the heaps. Excellent results have been obtained using a kind of square wooden bin made from planks; the material to be composted consists of all kinds of vegetable refuse, but no hard woody material.

Put the material into the bin to a depth of 6 in., and tread it well. Then sprinkle on fish manure, seawood manure or dried poultry manure at the rate of 3 oz per square yard. If very dry, water it in – the quantity of water to be added is controlled by the dampness of the material composted; it should never be sodden, but just moist. (Water should never ooze out of the composting material when squeezed in the hand.) Continue in this way. At every fourth layer hydrated lime should be applied at 2 oz per square yard in the first year of composting. After the first year or two no lime is needed, as calcium will be produced by the organic matter from the garden.

It is convenient to have the fish fertilizer or other activator in a dustbin near the heap. An artificial rain sprinkler on the end of a hose makes it a simple matter to water the heap if the weather is very dry. Some gardeners have to use baled straw for making compost, in which case plenty of water is necessary – it takes 800 to 1000 gallons to water 1 ton of straw properly.

At the end of 5–6 months, depending on the material composted and the time of the year (quicker in spring and summer, slower in winter when the temperature is low), the compost should be ripe – a dark, sweet smelling, powdery substance, containing all the necessary plant foods and with the necessary glutinous quality to bind the soil particles together. (It is also possible to use bottled liquid seaweed manure to bind the soil together. Use this instead of fish manure or dried poultry manure.) The soil therefore does not get blown away; it provides a medium for the soil bacteria to work upon, and so plant food is produced in the right condition to be absorbed by the roots and utilised by the plants.

If you cannot make a wooden bin, make the bin of some other material. It means that the outside 1-ft strip of material may not be properly composted, but it can be cut off when the compost is used and put on the bottom of a new heap.

If you have no suitable bin, heaps made in the open can be surrounded by plastic sheets, but they are never as successful. They take longer to mature, the winds lower the temperature and heavy rains may produce excess moisture. Choose a well-drained, sheltered spot for the heap and, if possible, start with a layer of ripened compost, straw or animal manure. Build in the same way as in the bin, using fish manure or seaweed manure as an activator. A 3-in. thickness of brittle material, such as straw and the dead stems of herbaceous plants, should be sandwiched, if possible, between layers of fresh green material such as grass mowings and cabbage leaves. Where a large quantity of green material is to be composted, it should be allowed to wilt first, otherwise the water content of the heap may be too high and an acid slime will be produced, excluding air and retarding the work of the bacteria.

While making the heap, cover it with sacks to keep in heat and moisture. Protect it if possible from excessive rain, and when the heap is finished put on a 2-in. layer of soil.

To test the condition of the compost, make a hole with a trowel in the side of the heap. If it is slimy, wet and sour-smelling it will be as well to strip off the covering, turn the heap and add drier material and a sprinkling of lime. If it is brittle and smells musty, either add diluted liquid manure or water or, if possible, turn the heap during the rain. The compost is ready for use when it has a pleasant, earthy smell and is brownish-black in colour and powdery.

3 Warming, sowing and ventilating

Soil warming

Gardeners who have not used cloches before cannot believe the difference that they can make to germination, and in consequence to seed-saving. If the cloches are put into position 10 days or a fortnight before sowing the seed, the soil is warmed and the surface can be got down to an extraordinarily fine tilth; a much higher percentage of seed germination is then obtained. (The packet may state that the germination percentage is as high as 80 per cent, but remember that germination tests are done under ideal conditions, and with cold, damp, a poor seedbed and so on, germination may easily be reduced to 30 or 40 per cent.)

Because of the soil-warming properties of cloches, seed-sowing is possible in the winter months. At the Horticultural Training College, good results cannot be guaranteed from outside sowing in October, January and February, and yet regular sowings of certain vegetables are made year after year with guaranteed success under cloches or Access frames.

It is of *vital importance*, however, to get the glass or plastic into position 7–10 days before sowing, particularly in the winter.

Electrical soil heating

The soil can be heated electrically under the cloches. A transformer is needed to reduce the usual voltage to 18–20 volts; use galvanized wire as the heating element, and bury it 5 in deep in the soil. Because the voltage is low there is no danger of a shock, and there is no chance of electric current being wasted. It is convenient to switch on the electric current in the evening and switch it off in the morning, except of course during frosty periods when the heat may be left on all the time. The temperature of the soil can be increased in this way by about 10 degrees.

The disadvantage of electrical soil warming is that the soil above dries out, and it may be necessary to water the ground under the cloches every 2 or 3 days if the plants are to grow properly. This involves spending time moving cloches. Northern gardeners, however, may like the idea because with artificial soil heating it is possible to have crops as early as in the south.

Soil heating is often used with cuttings or for forcing chicory, and in fact in some experiments made in the south chicory was ready for use in salads 3 weeks after it was planted under whitewashed cloches.

The electrical propagator

One adaptation of the soil-warming idea is the electrical seed propagator, which consits of two barn cloches mounted on a specially made timber container. The base of the box is filled with horticultural peat which is thoroughly damped beforehand. The heating element wire is then laid in rows on top of the peat and the specially constructed seed boxes (16 to one propagator) sit snugly just on top of the element.

When the electricity is switched on the element becomes warm and the No-Soil compost in the seed boxes is heated to about 60 degrees F. Many gardeners who have no greenhouse use this kind of propagator for raising plants of all kinds, and so get a flying start – annual flowering plants have been raised in this way, as well as tomatoes, marrows, cucumbers and melons. The propagator has been used for salad crops like radishes and mustard and cress, and is useful for striking chrysanthemums and dahlia cuttings and for starting off tubers such as begonias.

Saving seed

It always pays to purchase the best seed as some varieties are better than others, and some seed firms specialize in certain vegetables and flowers and have produced exclusive strains. If you don't start with good seed, how can you expect to produce a good crop?

The best seed may be more expensive, but if you use cloches it should go twice or three times as far. Seed under cloches should be sown extremely thinly. To ensure this sowing, it is a good plant to whiten small seeds with lime, so that they can be more easily seen. In cases where vegetables have to be eventually spaced out, 4, 5, 6 or 8 in. apart, sow the seed this distance apart, say three seeds at each position. If each of the seeds grows – as they usually do under cloches – then all that has to be done is to thin out to one. Sowing seeds in a continuous line in a drill is a tremendous waste of seed and, eventually, of seedlings.

Quick germination

Plants which germinate quickly are far less likely to bolt (i.e. go to seed), particularly in the case of endive and lettuce, than plants which are produced from seed which has germinated slowly. Experienced gardeners are most anxious to ensure immediate germination in the case of all their seeds, for nothing is more disheartening than sudden bolting just when plants should be ready for use. Cloches, of course, ensure quick germination.

Station sowing in a seedbed with seeds whitened with lime

Wind protection
Wind can do a tremendous amount of harm to plants. Not only does it buffet the leaves and cause physical injury, but in addition it brings about excessive transpiration with the result that the plants find difficulty in keeping the foliage turgid. This strains the roots and in due course dries out the soil.

Cloches give ideal protection against wind, especially those dreadful drying ground winds. The plants are undisturbed, no excessive transpiration takes place and the rate of growth and succulence are increased.

Saving space
For small seeds the drills should be very shallow, and for larger seeds, such as peas and beans, 2–3 in. deep. The lighter the soil the deeper the drills should be. Save space by arranging two rows of cloches close together whenever this is possible. A

Gardeners should always see that the crowns of growing plants are not too deep in soil or too far out of it

narrow alley should then be made between the next two rows, and in this way the plants can be tended with very little trouble.

Moving cloches

It is not as a result necessary to move the cloches at all for weeding, picking, thinning, etc., as the top sheet of glass on each cloche can be taken out and replaced. If you want to move the cloches to carry out some particularly difficult work, use this system. Moving the end cloches of the first row to the other end. After working on the area previously covered by this cloche (no. 1), cloche no. 2 should be moved forward to where no. 1 stood. The soil that was covered by no. 2 cloche can then be given its treatment and cloche no.3 moved forward one place as before. Cloche no. 1 then takes its place at the end of the row after all the cloches have been moved up one, as described.

The sunny situation

The function of the cloche is to trap sunshine – not to manufacture it. Always, therefore, try to have continuous cloches in a sunny situation. If the rows run east and west, instead of north and south, they will get the minimum amount of shade from the wires and the maximum amount of sun. Rows that run east and west seem to make the most of the sun in the late afternoon and early evening. It is more important, therefore, to have cloches running in this direction in the winter and early spring than it is in the summer.

Late and early sowing
Cloches allow seed-sowing to be carried out both early and late. They are useful when seeds are to be sown in June and July; with french beans, for instance, the protection they give enables the crop to go on producing tender pods until the end of October. From sowings made in the winter and early in the year, cloches ensure that the crops are available early, at a time when vegetables and flowers are scarce.

Thinning
It is a great mistake to grow plants too closely under cloches. Thinning, therefore, should be done early, so as to leave the best plants in position at the right distance apart. The root systems, as well as the parts of the plant above ground, will have plenty of room for development. After thinning, the soil along the rows must be firmed.

It is often economical to thin at two periods, in the first instance to half the distances ultimately intended to be left for the crop, and in the second instance so as to remove every other plant. The advantage of this method is that the plants at the second thinning are fit to use in the house and yet do not interfere with the permanent crop.

Intercropping
With larger cloches or Access frames, it is usually possible to intercrop – to arrange, for instance, that two rows of lettuces are produced on either side of a row of peas; or to have a row of spring onions sown in between two rows of lettuces. Another scheme is to have two of carrots on either side of a row of beetroot, while yet another is to have two rows of turnips on either side of a row of lettuces.

There intercropping schemes are usually carried out with barn cloches, which are wider and so cover more ground. With a little care and ingenuity schemes can be worked out to suit the particular garden or the demands of the individual.

Maturity
How long should cloches be left on each crop? The answer, of course, differs from district to district and from one cropping

scheme to another. There is no reason at all, provided the cloche is tall enough, why they should not be left in position over the crops until harvesting time. This is often done in the case of carrots, lettuces, beetroot, spinach, french beans, various flowers and so on. Where, however, the plant reaches the top of the cloche, and starts to press its leaves against the glass, the glass coverings should be removed altogether and the plant left to grow normally in the open.

Cloches can *start* all crops, and they can also mature most, if desired.

Ventilating

If the cloche has a ventilating handle it should be used to give extra ventilation to the ridge of the cloche in warm weather. From May to September cloches will almost always be kept permanently ventilated, and also during hot spells at other times. During the summer months, extra ventilation may be given during very hot weather by taking out the removable top sheet of glass or even by spacing the cloches so that they stand 1–2 in. apart. The ends of the rows should always be kept closed with sheets of glass or squares of wood or asbestos to prevent through draughts.

4 Cropping, standardization, continuity and watering

It is impossible to lay down hard-and-fast rules in regard to cropping, and it would not be advisable to do so. Some people feel that continuous cloches should be used only in a special part of the garden put aside for the purpose, and this is quite a good idea. They are, however, invaluable in any part of the garden. The great secret of their success is that they will fit over any row of plants at any time. They can thus hurry plants along, give protection from rain or frost, warm the soil and even help in controlling pests and diseases.

One of the most successful ways in which continuous cloches can be used is for the production of lettuces all the year round. Special hints on growing this crop appear in Chapter 10. Other crops depend greatly on personal preferences. If you are keen on tomatoes you will use a large number of tall cloches for this purpose. If you like sweet corn you will use barn cloches in great numbers to produce these plants much earlier than from ordinary outdoor sowings.

Sealing the ends
Having got the cloches into position it is always advisable, as I have said, to seal up the ends with squares of wood or sheets of glass. This prevents them from becoming funnels through which tremendous draughts of air can be blown. You can buy special wires to push into the ground which keep the squares of glass at the ends of the rows firmly in position. Alternatively, use bamboos or wooden stakes, with the tops securely tied to the handles of the cloches. By using the ends in this way, you make a low greenhouse covering the plants, with the necessary permanent ventilation assured through the slight opening along the ridge of each cloche and at the eaves of barn cloches.

It is always better to keep the ends closed the whole time, both in summer and winter; they should never be removed to give extra ventilation, which should be supplied by using the ventilating handle or by spacing out the cloches.

Flecking
In very bright sunshine certain plants, e.g. strawberries, cucumbers and aubergines, may need a little protection when ripening their fruits under continuous cloches. Make up a thick paste of lime and water, and use a large brush to flick a little paste on to the outside of the glass to produce a flecked or spotted effect. This breaks up the sun's rays and prevents scorching.

Standardization
There is a great advantage in having large numbers of cloches of the same size and trying to work to some standard in the garden. This makes it easier to transfer cloches from one crop to another, and to calculate rows, distances and the necessary cloche coverage required.

Continuity
Cloches should never be out of use. They can be removed from one crop that is getting too tall and transferred immediately to cover another crop that needs their help and protection.

Not only should they be used all the time, but they should always be in continuous rows, and experience has shown that the longer the rows, the better the crop. It is the cumulative effect of many cloches alongside each other that is so valuable. See that the rows are straight, and that the cloches fit against one another as closely as possible.

Wrapping
Cloches, when stood up on end, can be placed around plants to enclose or wrap them. Sometimes complete wrapping is not possible and then the cloches may be placed on end behind the plants to act as reflectors. In this way they give protection from wind (a very important point) and they ensure that the plant receives the maximum sun heat available.

Watering
It is most important that the soil is moist enough before seed is sown to be covered with cloches. It may be necessary, for instance, to give the ground a good soaking in the summer before it is dug over for cloche culture. Do the soaking before the ground is dug over, and not after. The moisture gets down properly if this is done, while, if you dig first of all, it will only

wet the top 3 or 4 in., and incidentally make the ground like a mud puddle.

However, most cloche sowings are made in the winter or early spring, when there will be plenty of moisture in the soil. It is important that the top 2–3 in. should not dry out and the incorporation of sedge peat can be very helpful.

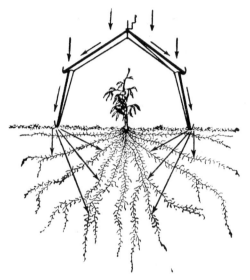

Distribution of water to the roots of plants grown under cloches.

Once the cloches have been put in position over the seeds, they should not be moved and it should not be necessary to water under the glass. After germination, the roots will reach down and obtain all the moisture they require. When rain falls, it percolates downwards and seeps sideways just below the surface, right to the centre of the cloches. The more organic matter there is in the soil, the faster the lateral movement of the water will be.

If, however, the surface soil dries out before germination, you must take out some of the movable top sheets of glass and water under the cloches with a rosed can. This won't be necessary if you prepared the soil properly at sowing time.

Once your plants are established, there is no need to water so long as there is sufficient rain outside the cloches. You must, however, keep the soil just outside the cloche rows hoed so that the rain is absorbed and does not merely run off the caked top surface. But if there is no rain, you will have to water your plants just as you would if there were no cloches over them. If you are using a can or hose, pour the water over the top of the cloches or hoe out channels on each side of a row of cloches and pour the water into them. Alternatively you can irrigate overhead with a square area, or circular, rainer.

5 Planning and strip cropping

A question often asked is: 'What is meant by the word *continuous?*' Briefly, the answer is (1) that the cloches are always used adjacent to one another in continuous lines, and (2) that they can be used continuously, that is to say all the year round. It is sensible to work out some plan which will ensure (a) that the cloches are in long straight rows, and (b) that they only have to be moved a couple of feet or so the moment their function on the original strip is over.

In my experience, you need 1 square yard of really well-composted ground for every 1-ft run of continuous cloches in use. At the Horticultural Training Centre we started off with a plot 20 ft long × 18 ft wide and used two 20-ft rows of cloches, one starting at one end of the plot and the other at the other end. We arranged for them to cover three different crops in the season, 1 ft being allowed in between the positions of each cloche line (see drawing).

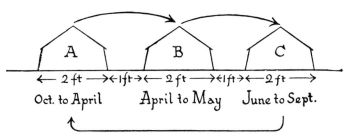

Three-strip rotation. This entails the minimum of cloche moving.

The cloches were first in position A, then they were moved on to B and later to C; the next move would be back to position B again and lastly back to strip A once more. The other set of cloches also worked in towards the centre and back again to the outside in the course of the 12 months. We then found that this apparently minimum area for cloches was insufficient because it was always useful to be able to move the cloches on to position D, even if only for a month or so, while the plants at B were coming to full maturity; so, instead of allowing a strip of land

18 ft wide, which is the absolute minimum for two rows of cloches, we developed a strip 30 ft wide, giving a little land to spare for an emergency. It can be seen that, whether the cloche rows are 20 ft or 30 ft long, the width of land must always be the same under this particular system.

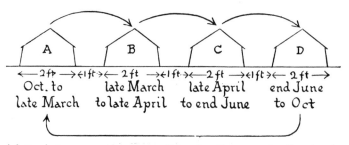

A *better but more complex system. It involves four moves in all and makes the maximum use of cloches with the minimum of labour.*

Three-strip system

What has been described is really the basic three-strip system of cloche cropping, and in an attempt to make it appear simple we have shown how the idea is worked out. It is quite possible to explain the three-strip system in a diagrammatic way, and here

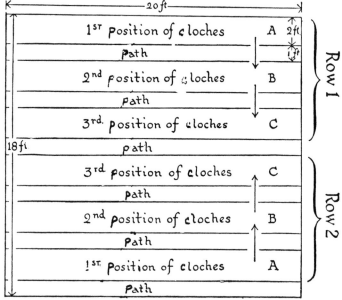

Three-strip system – working from the outside towards the middle. The paths are only trodden down earth.

the plan is to start with strip A, then move on to strip B and so to strip C for the summer, then to start back on strip A for the winter again; the last is a big move for cloches. The idea is to grow crops, say from the beginning of October until the middle of April, on A, and then to use strip B for the late spring crops, say the middle of April to the end of May, and strip C for the summer crops, such as cucumbers or melons, which may be from the third week of May until the end of September.

The disadvantage of the system, if you keep to the same land for cloches each year, is that you tend always to grow the same kind of crops on the same area of land; that is why I previously advised the use of extra ground so that, instead of moving back to the original A, you can start a new A on the other side of C if you wish.

Simple two-strip system

When you mention three strips, some people get agitated and think that the whole scheme is far too complicated – they say that they would rather not use cloches at all if they have to work out a scheme of this kind. If you feel like this, use the two-strip rotation, for there is nothing simpler. The idea is to start in October with the cloches on strip A and then in April move them on to strip B, 1 ft away. They stay there until the end of May, when they are moved back again to strip A, which by that time has been cleared of its crop and forked over, enriched with peat and plant foods, and is ready for the next crop.

The only thing to watch about this system is that the vegetable or flower which is grown on strip A must be one that can definitely be cleared by the end of May when the new crop will need to go into position.

Four- or five-strip system

As soon as you become interested in continuous cloches and fascinated by the results, you can try and work out more complicated rotations which will give just the results desired with the minimum amount of labour. Remember that cloches are not only used for flowers, salad plants and vegetables – they can also play their part in growing strawberries and raspberries. The more crops that are introduced into the general scheme the more interesting can the idea of strip rotation become. For instance strawberries need to be covered from, say, January to the end of May, and thus the use of cloches during that period cuts across the normal times advised for strip rotations.

Sit down with some squared paper in the winter and work out exactly how the cloches are going to be used. It is not worthwhile, for instance, to include parsnips, which do just as well without cloches, or Jerusalem artichokes which will yield heavily without any extra help. Use the cloches intelligently and, if you like, make little wooden scale models, lay them on the squared paper where they are going to be for the first period, and then move them on until the whole of your four- or five-strip cropping plan has been organized.

Take a typical example: strip A starts off with lettuce sown in October, and the cloches are moved on late in March to cover the early beet on strip B; the cloches are moved on to strip C where it is intended to grow, say, french beans or tomatoes, then, at the end of June when all fear of frost is past, to strip D where the summer crops will be, such as frame cucumbers or melons. Another move can be made if necessary in September to cover potatoes planted in August, with the idea of digging them at Christmas. This gives us our fifth strip.

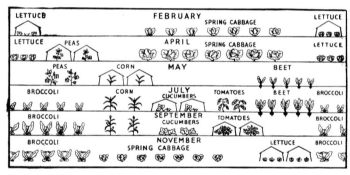

The four- or five-strip system

When, however, the fifth strip is adopted it is difficult to start off again with normal cropping for strip A, i.e. lettuces to be covered in October or spring cabbage which is sometimes covered in the north. But on the other hand, once the potatoes are dug at Christmastime it is possible to alter the rotation scheme and start with onions, celery and brassicas in January, and so the general planning of the strip cropping is altered slightly from year to year.

The four- or five-strip system, however, which the drawing shows is not only effective but simple to operate, and on the whole is the best of all the rotational cropping schemes I have planned.

Four-strip rotation with jam jars

You can get a flying start on some of the strips by introducing the 'jam jar' method. The plan is to start with broad beans on strip A – these will be sown in October and covered until late March. The cloches will then go on to strip B where it is intended to sow annuals for use as cut flowers, with a row of beetroot on either side. The next move is on to strip C to cover marrows, but it won't be possible to de-cloche the annuals until late April; as this will be rather late to start off marrows,

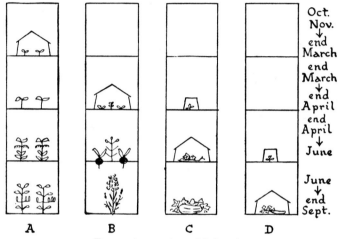

Four-strip rotation with jam jars

upturned jam jars are used to cover the seeds of marrows sown *in situ* about the end of March or the beginning of April. The marrows then grow well and when the cloches are moved from strip B late in April they go over marrows which have developed considerably by that time.

Now we have strip D to bear in mind; once again we want early cucumbers and so we sow seeds *in situ* again about the beginning of May, and cover them with upturned jam jars. The plants are then growing well by the beginning of June, when the barn cloches can be removed from strip C to go over the cucumbers on D. The diagram shows how the scheme works in principle.

Double-cloche method

It saves time and makes for maximum efficiency if the strips of land can be wide enough to accommodate two rows of cloches running side by side, separated only by a 3- or 4-in. width;

under this scheme 18 in. should be left at the side of the pair of cloches instead of 1 ft as advised for the single-cloche line system. Therefore, there are two rows of cloches 2 ft wide, equalling 4 ft, a 4-in. space in between them, and then 18 in. for the pathway. This makes 5 ft 10 in. in all, and so 6 ft is usually allowed per strip.

If you adopt this system, the scheme is to have a double row of cloches with an adjacent strip of the same width carrying no crop; then a third strip with a double row of cloches, probably protecting a similar crop to the first strip; after this a fourth strip bare, and so on right across the available land. The pairs of cloches are very easy to move together – you just lift one cloche with one hand and one with the other, and move the two together to their new bit of ground. When the crop on the first strip is cleared, the land is once again manured and prepared for the third crop when the pairs of cloches will be moved back to the first strip once more. This is a simple method and there is no doubt that using the two rows of cloches together does save room and time.

Crops and cloche periods

Details as to how the various crops should be grown are given in separate chapters, together with suggestions as to when the cloches should be used. It should not therefore take the reader long to work out strip rotations to suit his own particular needs, but it may be as well to divide up the bulk of the crops into periods of sowing to give pointers to help with planning. The four main divisions are: (1) early spring, (2) late spring, (3) summer and (4) autumn.

Early Spring

List of crops	Harvesting starts
Onion plants	April
Lettuces	April
Peas	May
Turnips	May
Carrots	May
Radishes	March
Beetroot	June
Annuals	May
Spring cabbage	March

Late Spring

List of crops	*Harvesting starts*
French beans	June
Marrows	Mid-June
Sweet corn	July
Tomatoes	July
Runner beans	July
Ridge cucumbers	July

Summer

Frame cucumbers	July
Melons	August
Late tomatoes	August
Aubergines	September
Capsicums	August

August

Endive	October
Autumn lettuce	November
August-planted potatoes	Christmas
Tomato fruit ripening	Until end of November
Sweet peas	End of May
Annuals	End of May
July-sown peas	October–November
July-sown french beans	October–November

CLOCHE COVERING FOR ODD PERIODS There are a number of crops which don't easily fit into a normal two-, three- or four-strip cropping scheme – gardeners using them must work out special schemes to keep the cloches in continual use.

Crops	*Cloches in use*	*Harvesting starts*
Strawberries	January–June	Late May
Violets	September–early March	February
Polyanthus	December–March	February
Asparagus	January–April	Cutting in March
Carnations	May–July	August
Onion ripening	July–August	September

Cauliflower plants	October–November	*March
Cabbage and sprout plants	January–March	*March
Bulbs	From when growth shows until stems need extra height	

*These crops are of course next planted out in the open where they are to mature.

6 Root crops

There is nothing to be gained in growing parsnips, swedes or maincrop turnips under cloches or Access frames, though in the north it has been found worthwhile to start these root crops under cloches so that sowing may be done earlier. This is particularly necessary in the case of parsnips. Cloches are, however, ideal for bringing along quick crops of the early types of carrots, turnips and beetroot. They can also be used to start off any root crop, and on occasions are invaluable for kohlrabi, salsify, scorzonera and Hamburg parsley.

Beetroot

Beetroot may be divided roughly into three classes: the round, the tankard and the long beet. In the case of the round beet, two further divisions may be made – the earlier and the main crops.

Cloches are generally used for the earliest, the gardener aiming to produce several crops of roots about the size of a tennis ball or even smaller. These are pulled purposely while young and fresh, when they are particularly delicious. Several sowings may be made throughout the season.

There is no reason at all why cloches should not be used either to warm the strip of land where the seed for main crops is to be sown, or to cover up the rows until the leaves touch the top of the glass tents.

SOILS AND MANURES   The lightest soils suit beetroot best, though they will do well on heavy clays if they are lightened by digging in sand, powdery sedge peat, flue dust, etc., and if the soil is dressed with lime.

Large quantities of fresh farmyard manure should not be dug in, for this causes the roots to fork. Composted seaweed has proved an excellent manure for beetroot and may be used at one barrowload to 10 square yard. In addition, fork into the top 3 or 4 in. a good fish manure, meat and bone meal or any complete fertilizer with an organic base at 3 or 4 oz to the square yard. On very sandy soil give salt in addition, at the rate of 2 oz to the square yard.

SOWING THE SEED   Under cloches the first sowing should be made at the end of March or the beginning of April. The roots will then be ready to use at the beginning of June; one row under large tent cloches, two rows 12 in. apart under low barns.

Sowings may then be made at fortnightly intervals if required; the last sowing should be made about the second week of July, and the roots will be ready in September. These may be kept throughout the winter and stored in sand or ashes. The drills should be 1½ in. deep.

THINNING   When the plants are 3 in. high, thin to 4 in. apart, and then, when the roots are the size of golf balls, thin to 8 in. apart. The later thinnings may be eaten.

TRANSPLANTING   It is possible to transplant round varieties of beetroot seedlings if it is done when they are young enough. They must be watered well, however, every day until well established.

HARVESTING   There is no difficulty in pulling roots grown under cloches. In fact, they are much easier to pull up than those grown out of door in the normal way. Care should be taken, however, not to bruise them, or bleeding may occur.

Before storing, the leaves should be cut or twisted off 1 in. above the roots – throw them on the compost heap to rot down as manure.

VARIETIES

Boltardy	An early round type which does not go to seed easily.
Crimson Ball	Good flavour.
Detroit New Globe	Entirely free from disfiguring white rings.
Detroit	Fine colour.
Formanova	Cylindrical, deep red, delicious.

Carrots

Under cloches there is no difficulty in having carrots almost all the year round.

SOILS AND MANURES   Carrots prefer a cultivated, sandy loam, and heavy soil should be improved by adding sandy or gritty material and plenty of fine sedge peat. It is better on clay soils to grow the shorter-rooted types.

Always put the cloches or Access frames into position a fortnight before sowing the seed, so that the soil will break down into the fine tilth necessary for this crop. Fork in lightly a good fertilizer with an organic base, at the rate of 4 oz to the square yard. Do not dig in fresh farmyard manure, which causes the roots to fork.

SOWING THE SEED   The drills should be 1-in. deep and about 9 in. apart, depending on the type of carrot grown and the cloches used. To ensure specially thin sowing, mix powdery horticultural peat or dry earth with the seed in equal proportions beforehand.

Early types can be sown 5 in. apart – i.e. four rows under low barn cloches.

Carrots and lettuce intercropping under Access frames

A good system is to sow a row of carrots in between two rows of lettuce under cloches. Another is to have two rows of carrots on either side of a central row of lettuce. Two rows will fit quite well under the large tent type of cloche, or four rows under the low barns.

The months to sow are January, February, August, September and October.

THINNING   If the sowing has been done properly, i.e. thinly enough, there should be no need to thin. However, where necessary, the plants should be thinned to 1 in. or so apart in the case of the short varieties, but to 6 in. apart in the case of the main crops.

TRANSPLANTING   Believe it or not, carrots may be transplanted when they are very tiny, but they do not transplant well on the whole.

HARVESTING   The roots may be pulled as desired and stored in sand or dry earth in a shed. The tops should be cut off first.

If cloches are used, little storage will be necessary, for, even in the depth of winter, roots usually pull up quite easily.

PESTS   The great pest of carrots is carrot fly, but under cloches the early roots are usually pulled before the eggs are even laid. With later sowings the cloches seem to keep the flies away.

VARIETIES

Chantenay Red Cored	A good variety for August sowing.
Guerande Early Gem	For the earliest sowing of the year.
James' Scarlet Intermediate	A first-class variety to sow in February as a main crop.
Nantes Express	An excellent type for cloche work.
Perfect Gem	Similar to Early Gem.

Turnips

The main function of cloches in connection with turnips is to produce delicious tennis-ball-sized roots almost all the year round. In the open the roots have a tendency to run to seed, and are usually badly attacked by the flea beetle. Under cloches they seldom suffer from either.

SOILS AND MANURES   The early-maturing types of turnips will do well on almost all soils, except very shallow ones.

Do not manure heavily with farmyard manure, but fork sedge peat into the top 3 in. at ½ lb to the square yard and, in addition, apply a fertilizer with an organic base, such as a good fish manure or a meat and bone meal at 4–5 oz per square yard.

SOWING THE SEED   The first sowing should be made in February, with the drills drawn out 1½ in. deep and 8–12 in. apart, depending on the cloches used. Two rows fit quite well under large tent cloches, and three rows under low barn cloches.

Further sowings may be made each month until the end of July. It is then that winter turnips should be sown, with the drills 12 in. apart and the seed spaced out, if possible, 9 in. apart. This allows two rows to be sown under low barn cloches, one under large tent cloches.

THINNING   The plants should be thinned to 6 in. apart when they are 1 in. high. It is most important not to allow the leaves of one root to touch the next in the early stages, so thinning must be done early and rigorously. The winter turnip sowings should be thinned to 6 in. apart when 2 in. high. A further thinning has to be done to 1 ft apart as soon as the roots are fit to use.

HARVESTING   The roots should be pulled when they are young and fresh, before they get coarse.

Winter turnips must be kept under cloches or Access frames throughout the winter, and if the weather is exceptionally frosty it may be necessary to cover the cloches with a little straw or bracken. The roots can then be pulled at any time.

VARIETIES

Early White Milan	A pure white.
Early White Stone	Good early variety.
Golden Ball	Small topped, yellow flesh.
Manchester Market	Flesh firm and white.
Snowball	Heavy cropping, delicious.

Parsnips

Parsnips may be started under cloches if necessary, allowing earlier sowings to be made in the north and also ensuring almost perfect germination. Sow in February. Arrange the rows 18 in. apart and the plants 9 in. apart in the rows; sow in drills 1½ in. deep. This means one row per ten-cloche row.

Remove the cloches directly the leaves touch the sides.

VARIETIES
Shallow soils:

Leda	A heavy cropper, slender roots.

Deeper soils:

Avonresister	Clearer and smoother skin than other varieties. Free from canker.

Swedes
Swedes may, like parsnips, be started under cloches to give them a good send-off. Sow the seed in drills 18 in. apart and 1 in. deep; under cloches sow early in May. This means one row per ten-cloche row. Aim to thin out the plants to 1 ft apart. Remove the cloches when the leaves touch the sides.

VARIETY
    Purple Top   Roots well shaped, good colour.

Kohlrabi
This is similar to turnip, but has a nuttier flavour. Sow early in March; further sowings may be made every fortnight until the beginning of August. Aim at rows 18 in. or 2 ft apart. Thin the plants to 6 in. apart. Remove the cloches when the plants get too big for them.

VARIETY
    White Vienna   Used for midsummer sowings.

Salsify
Salsify is a delicious, unusual root crop which may be started under continuous cloches. Treat as for carrots. Sow seed early April. The drills should be 1 ft apart and 1 in. deep. Thin to 8 in. apart and 1 in. deep. Thin to 8 in. apart. Remove the cloches in early June.

VARIETY
    Mammoth Vegetable Oyster   Delicate and sweet flavour.

7 Peas and beans

All members of the pea and bean family prove excellent crops for growing under cloches or Access frames. They are valuable because they add nitrogen to the soil and leave it in a better condition than when the seed was sown. The ash from the burned, dried tops of broad beans is very rich in potash.

Runner beans, when sown under cloches, often come into cropping 3 weeks earlier than ordinary out-of-door sowings. They enable the gardener in the north to sow beans 3 weeks or a month earlier than he would normally.

Broad beans
Seed sown in January under cloches or frames produces plants which come into cropping quite as early as normal November sowings in open ground. There is no risk of loss by frost. Also, by delaying sowings until January or February, the ground can be used more advantageously for winter crops such as lettuce, spinach or radishes.

SOILS AND MANURES   The broad bean is happy on almost any soil. Properly composted vegetable refuse should be forked in at the rate of one good barrowload to 10 square yard. In addition, rake into the top 2 in. a fertilizer with an organic base, such as a good fish manure or meat and bone meal, at 5 oz to the square yard.

SOWING THE SEED   Drills should be drawn out 5 in. wide and 3 in. deep; sow a double row of beans in the drill, zig-zag fashion, so that the seeds are 6 in. apart. After covering over, put a large cloche into position, and sow another row down the centre of the next cloche row, which should be as close as possible to the original one. An alley should then be left for the next pair of cloches, and so on. As the tent cloches are not going to be left in position all through the life of the beans, there should be no difficulty in having two single rows of broad beans per 'large' cloche row.

51

Make the first sowing in January and further sowings in February and early March. In every case start the beans under cloches, which are removed when the plants are 6 in. high and, if available, taller barn cloches substituted. From the January sowings it should be possible at the end of April to remove the cloches altogether and use them for another crop. A little more space may be left between the cloches during flowering, so as to ensure perfect fertilization.

Two or three beans should be sown at the end of each row, so that, should any gaps appear, the plants that result from these end-of-row sowings can be used for filling up. Broad beans transplant quite well.

HARVESTING   Pick the pods regularly when young.

PESTS   The earliest broad beans under cloches escape the black fly. But with later sowing keep a close watch, and immediately there are any signs give a thorough spraying with liquid derris. It is not necessary to pinch out the tops to control black fly.

VARIETIES
    Imperial White Long Pod   A tall-growing variety bearing enormous pods.
    Imperial White Windsor   Very excellent flavour.
    Masterpiece Green Long Pod   Bears large, well-filled pods of good flavour.

French beans (dwarf or kidney beans)
The french bean comes into cropping earlier than its cousin, the runner bean, and withstands drought possibly better than any other vegetable crop.

SOILS AND MANURES   The french bean prefers a light soil to a heavy one. Prepare the ground as advised for broad beans; as lime is a necessity for all members of this family, after forking in organic fertilizer apply hydrated lime to the surface of the ground, at 4–7 oz per square yard, depending on the acidity of the soil.

SOWING THE SEED   Drills should be prepared as for broad beans, 2 in. deep, and the seed spaced out in these 4 in. apart. Rows may vary from 2 to 3 ft apart. It is better on the whole to have one row per cloche row.

The first sowing should be done at the end of March, and from this sowing beans can be picked in June. Sowings may be made once a fortnight until July if necessary. The July sowing produces delicious pods in October.

The rows should first of all be covered with cloches. When the plants are well grown, the cloches should be removed.

GENERAL NOTES   If the weather is particularly dry, it may be necessary to take out shallow drills on each side of the row of cloches and give these a thorough soaking from time to time. Overhead irrigation is also useful.

In the case of the summer sowings, it is possible to leave the pods on and allow them to ripen, when the beans may be shelled out to be stored and used as haricot beans in the winter.

VARIETIES

Flair	A dwarf variety for those with low cloches only.
Pencil Pod Wax	Stringless and fibreless, useful for summer sowings.
The Prince	Very good for cloche work.
Processor	Good for early work, round oval stringless pods.

Runner beans

Cloches here make all the difference, for they make it possible to sow seed early without any fear that the young plants will be ruined by frost. Runner beans started in this way are usually 3 weeks ahead of those grown without protection.

SOILS AND MANURES   Whatever the soil, it should be well worked. Properly composted organic waste should be forked in at the rate of one good barrowload to 10 square yard. This should be incorporated in the top 3 or 4 in. of soil. In addition, a fortnight or so before the seed is sown, an organic fertilizer should be raked into the top 2 in., at the rate of 4–5 oz to the square yard. Just before seed-sowing, hydrated lime should be applied to the surface of the ground, at 3–5 oz. to the square yard.

SOWING THE SEED   The seed should be sown in drills spaced 9 in. apart. The first sowing should be made about the middle of March in the south, though in the north it is better to wait until the second week in April. As a result, beans are ready to use from mid-July onwards, whereas from ordinary sowings they are not usually ready until August.

GENERAL NOTES   As soon as the plants are ready to climb, the cloches may be removed and stick or string supports arranged for them. If you want to grow runners on the dwarf system, the tops of the plants should be pinched back when they are 18 in. high, and further pinching back should take place when the subsequent growths are 18 in. long. In this case, after the cloches are removed they may be placed on the weather side of the plants to give a certain amount of further protection for a fortnight or so. The alternative is to grow a dwarf variety of runner bean like Hammond's Dwarf.

HARVESTING   Pick the beans regularly when they are ready, and a continuous supply will be assured until the autumn.

VARIETIES

Hammond's Dwarf	An early variety, particularly suited to cloches.
Kelvedon Marvel	A better bean than Princeps and almost as early.
Scarlet Emperor Improved	A heavy cropper.
Streamline	Produces particularly long pods.

Peas

Generally speaking, some sort of pea-guards must be used with outdoor sowings of peas, as birds are very troublesome. Under cloches, of course, these are not necessary. The plants are also protected from being beaten down by wind or rain, and so with the dwarf varieties no staking is required. Peas can be wholly grown under cloches until they are harvested, if dwarf varieties are chosen and taller cloches are available.

SOILS AND MANURES   Peas will grow on almost any soil. They dislike acidity, however, and so liming is a necessity.

Composted vegetable refuse should be forked in 3 or 4 in. deep at the rate of one good barrowload to 10 square yard. In addition, a good organic fertilizer should be raked into the top 2 in. at 4 oz to the square yard. Wood ashes, if available, may be applied at 3–4 oz to the square yard.

SOWING THE SEED   Put the cloches in position a week or 10 days before sowing. Draw out drills 2 in. deep and 4 in. wide, and space the seeds out 2 in. apart, zig-zag or staggered. Cover with soil, firm and cover with cloches, making sure to close the ends with sheets of glass. Make this first sowing in November or January. From January sowings the pods are ready to pick from mid-May onwards.

To prevent mice from getting the seeds, put down back-breaking traps baited with marrow seeds. These go easily under the cloches.

Further sowings may be made once a fortnight, if necessary, until the beginning of July. The earliest-maturing varieties should be sown then, so as to get good pickings in September and early October. Such sowings usually follow early potatoes or early cauliflowers. Make sure that the soil is damp before sowing the seed, and give it a good flooding beforehand if necessary.

The distance from one row to another depends, of course, on the variety sown. Roughly speaking, give the variety half its height on either side of it. Thus a 3-ft variety needs an 18-in. space on either side, and the next row another 18 in. on either side, making 3 ft in all.

GENERAL NOTES   It is possible, where peas are being grown throughout under the largest cloches, to have a catch-crop of cabbage, lettuce or radishes on either side of the row.

Good waterings may be given from time to time as advised for french beans.

HARVESTING   Pick regularly – making sure not to miss any pods – directly they are ready; otherwise cropping is impeded.

VARIETIES
Dwarf:

English Wonder	Dwarf, dark, a week earlier than Kelvedon, 1½ ft.
Kelvedon Wonder	Dark-green-podded, 1½ ft.
Kwartella	Excellent cropper, fine flavour, 2½ ft.
Progress No. 9	Good cropper, 1½ ft.

Very early:

Meteor	Very heavy cropper, 1 ft, probably the best cloche variety.

Early:
<table>
<tr><td>Early Onward</td><td>Stump-podded, 2 ft.</td></tr>
<tr><td>Gradus</td><td>Fine pods, 3 ft.</td></tr>
<tr><td>Histon Mini</td><td>Well-filled pods, good cropper, 12 in., excellent for cloches.</td></tr>
</table>

Maincrop:

Onward	Highly recommended, 2½ ft.

Sugar peas (mange tout)

Sugar peas should be grown in exactly the same was as peas. The pods, however, should be pulled when young to be cooked whole, without cutting. They can either be served hot, or cold and shredded in salads.

VARIETY

Dwarf Sweet Green   Heavy cropper.

8 The Cabbage Family

Cloches are particularly useful for raising healthy young plants early in the year. Brussels sprouts, for instance, can be produced in a hardy condition from January sowings. Early summer cabbage, such as Primata, can also be got in earlier. Cloches are most useful for covering spring cabbages early in the year, especially in the north; in this way they are produced earlier and none will be lost.

Broccoli

With cloches or Access frames you can protect broccoli in the winter, especially if the plants are bent over towards the north. This can be done by taking out a spadeful of soil on the north side of the plant, heeling the plant over, and then putting the soil on the back of the plant. This, however, is rather an uneconomical way of using cloches, and would probably not be followed except in special circumstances in the north.

It is possible to produce beautiful white curds from November of one year to the middle of June the following year.

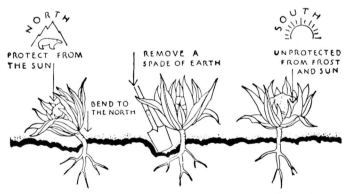

Protect broccoli in winter by heeling plants over to the north

SOILS AND MANURES Broccoli prefers firm soil, and so should follow a crop that has been well manured. Light, sandy soils may have composted vegetable refuse forked in at the rate of one barrowload per 10 square yard. This should be incorporated 4 in. down. Firming, however, must be done afterwards.

Rake into the top 2 or 2 in. fish manure at 3–4 oz to the square yard and sulphate of potash at ½ oz to the square yard. If these are unobtainable, use wood ashes at 3 oz per square yard.

SOWING THE SEED   Sow seed under cloches early in March in drills ½ in. deep; upturned glass jam jars suit seedlings quite well. Seed rows may be as close as 9 in. apart. Whiten the seeds and space them out 1 in. apart for, under cloches, every seed grows.

It is really only the earliest sowings that need covering with cloches. The later sowings can be sown in the open.

PLANTING   Plant after such crops as french beans, early potatoes, early carrots or early peas. Arrange them 2 ft square. If the weather is dry, put plenty of water in the holes at planting time. Firm well.

GENERAL NOTES   Hoe regularly. Watch for cabbage root maggot. Use squares of tarred felt around the stems of the plants to prevent this pest.

HARVESTING   Cut directly the curds are ready. If too many ripen at a time, pull them up and hang them by their heels in a shed.

VARIETIES (FOR AUTUMN)
   Knight's Protecting   Perhaps the most delicious.
   Walcheren Winter   More suitable for the north.

NB There are other varieties, such as St Agnes for late December, Early Feltham for mid-January, Armado April for April, Armado May for May, and Late Queen for June, but these can normally be sown out of doors, though cloche protection will prevent damage by birds.

Sprouting broccoli
Sprouting broccoli is a very hardy vegetable. By growing several varieties it is possible to cut from late September to the beginning of April.

SOILS AND MANURES   As advised for broccoli.

SOWING THE SEED   Sow in April as advised for broccoli.

PLANTING   Plant out 2 ft square when ready, on any land available.

HARVESTING   Cut the flower shoots found growing in the axils of the leaves to less than two-thirds of their length, and as a result more shoots will be thrown out on the same stem. Do not cut the main heads until all the sprouting tips have been harvested.

VARIETIES

Calabrese	Usually used in September, needs 2½ ft square.
Early Half Tall	Produces large sprouts of excellent quality up to Christmas.
Early Purple Sprouting	Cuts in February and March.
Late Purple Sprouting	Excellent in April.

Brussels sprouts

SOWING THE SEED   Brussels sprouts seeds should be sown as advised for broccoli at the end of March. It is a good plan first to whiten the seeds with lime to make thin sowing easier. Thin out when 2 in. high to 3 in. apart under further cloches.

Plant the young plants in the open ground at the end of April or early May, 3 ft × 3 ft. It should be possible as a result to harvest the first sprouts late in August.

GENERAL NOTES   The sprouts should be picked from the bottom of the plant first.

PESTS AND DISEASES   Look out for the blue bug or blue aphis and spray with liquid derris or nicotine immediately it is seen.

COVERING   Tent cloches are quite suitable for sprouts and are usually in use during the months of January, February and March.

VARIETIES

Irish Elegance	Tall uniform, heavy cropping.
King Arthur Prince Askold	Two excellent F1 hybrid varieties.

Cabbages

Cloches are useful mainly for spring cabbages, and to produce very early summer cabbages. They need not be used for winter cabbages or savoys.

SOILS AND MANURES   For summer cabbages fold in old properly composted vegetable refuse at the rate of one barrowload to 10 square yard. In addition, rake in lightly a complete organic fertilizer at 3 oz per square yard. For spring cabbages do not fork in compost but rely on the organic matter left behind by the previous crop – often potatoes. In spring, however – say February – give blood or soot along the rows at 3 oz to the yard run.

Lime is always necessary. It should be applied on the surface of the ground before the plants are put out, at about 5–7 oz of hydrated lime per square yard.

GENERAL NOTES   *Early summer cabbages.* Sow the seed in January or February under cloches. Prepare a fine seed bed. Drills should be ½ in. deep and the seed sown as close as 9 in. apart. Keep the plants under cloches until they are well established. Put them out in the open with 18 in. between the rows and 18 in. between the plants. Hearts are usually ready for use in May. *Spring cabbages.* Normally, spring cabbage seed is sown in July and transplanted in September or October. Under cloches seed-sowing may be delayed until September and the plants either over-wintered in cloches or put out in the open in early November, spaced out 18 in. × 12 in.

This sowing under cloches needs only be undertaken when normal July sowings were forgotten or were not possible. Cloches may be put over the plants in January to give the necessary protection and so produce spring cabbages much earlier. It is possible in this way to have a supply of good hearts in March.

VARIETIES
Spring:

Clucas' First Early 218	Probably the earliest variety of cabbage known.
Durham Early	Follows above. Delicious hearts.

Summer:

Greyhound	Pointed hearts, few outer leaves, good flavour, early maturing.
Primo	A lovely round cannon ball.

Cauliflowers

Cloches and Access frames are useful with cauliflowers, for they enable the seeds to be sown much earlier and so curds are fit to cut early in the summer.

SOILS AND MANURES   As advised for cabbages. Firm soil if necessary, as for broccoli.

SOWING THE SEED   The first sowing should be made late in August or early September, under cloches. Sow thinly, and winter the plants under the cloches, putting them out in the open early in April in a sheltered part of the garden. It is sometimes necessary to give extra protection to these plants by covering the cloches with sacking during very frosty periods.

The next sowing should be made in January and February. When the plants come through they should be pricked out 4 in. apart under further cloches, which should be put in position over the ground a fortnight beforehand to warm the soil. The plants that result should be put out early in April.

The third sowing should be made under cloches late in March, with drills ½ in. deep. Sow the seed thinly – spaced, say, to 1 in. apart. Thin out and transplant to 3 in. apart, finally planting in the open when land is available.

With all these sowings it is necessary to keep down club root disease and take precautions against cabbage root maggot when planting out.

PLANTING   Autumn sowings are often planted 1 ft square in March in a sheltered position. It is possible to cover with barn cloches if you want very early cauliflowers.

From the later sowings the plants should be put out 2½ ft apart and 2 ft apart in the rows. Aim always at transplanting early, before the plants get too big.

You can always obtain succession by planting out further batches without cloche protection, or to remove the cloches after a week or two of covering.

It is most important never to transplant cauliflowers too deeply, or they will go blind.

GENERAL NOTES   When the plants start to curd out of doors, bend one or two of the inner leaves over the 'flower' to prevent it turning yellow.

VARIETIES

Autumn sowing:

All-the-Year-Round	A compact grower
Alpha	An early, well-protected type.

January and February sowings:

Canberra	Does not seed easily.
Focus	Lovely white curds.
Snowball	A later All-the-Year-Round.

There are later varieties of cauliflower which can be sown in the open, in April or early May, and need not be covered by cloches.

Kales and savoys

Kales and savoys may be raised under cloches if necessary, but it is seldom done. Where early kales are desired under cloches, the seed can be put in late in February or early in March.

Savoys are really a type of hardy winter cabbage. The seed should be sown in early March, and the hearts should be ready to cut in September.

In Scotland, cloches have proved excellent for protecting winter savoys and other greens.

9   Other vegetables

Onions
There is no doubt that to get the heaviest crops and largest bulbs it is necessary to sow onion seed under glass and to transplant the seedlings later. Cloches are ideal for this purpose, for under them the hardiest little plants are produced, and, as result, attack by onion fly are few and far between.

SOILS AND MANURES   Onions do best on a rich, sandy loam. They will do well, however, on a much heavier soil, providing this is opened up by the addition of sand, burned soil or other finely divided gritty matter.

The soil should be forked over shallowly some time before seed-sowing, to allow it to settle down. Properly composted vegetable waste should be incorporated at least 3 or 4 in. deep, at the rate of one good barrowload per 12 square yard, and in addition the following organic fertilizers may be forked into the top 2 in.; steamed bone flour at 4 oz to the square yard, wood ashes at ½ lb to the square yard, soot at ¼ lb to the square yard and, if available, dried powdered poultry manure at 3 oz to the square yard. Instead of all these, an organic proprietary fertilizer containing about 7 per cent potash, 7 per cent phosphates and 4 per cent nitrogen may be used.

It is most important to firm the soil before sowing the seed. This may be done either by treading or rolling, but never when the soil is sticky.

All these preparations refer to the land where the onions are to be planted out.

SOWING THE SEED   There are two main periods for seed-sowing: in the autumn and in the spring. With autumn sowings there are two sub-divisions: for salads and for early summer bulbs. Different varieties have to be grown in each case.
Autumn sowing. In the case of salad onions, no special preparation of the ground need be carried out.

It is only necessary to choose soil that was well manured for a previous crop, such as potatoes. The seed should be sown in the latter part of July or the beginning of August. On the whole, the farther north the earlier the sowing. The rows should be 9 in. apart and the drills 1 in. deep. Cover with cloches or Access frames as soon as these are available from other crops – say early in October. The onions, as a result, are pulled fresh for salad purposes in the spring.

For the early summer 'bulbing' onions, the same rules hold good, except that the rows should be 1 ft apart. The plants that result, however, are thinned in the spring, the thinnings being transplanted 12 in. between the rows and 6 in. between the plants. Cloches may be put over these rows if particularly early crops are desired. Otherwise the cloches may be released for other crops.

Spring Sowing. If you are going to plant out to get the heaviest bulbs, you should sow in shallow drills in January in rows 4–6 in. apart under any cloches. The sowing should be done very thinly. It is even worthwhile spacing the seeds out to 1 in. apart, having whitened them with lime first of all so that they can easily be seen. Plant four rows 5 in. apart under a barn-like cloche and, say, two rows 6 in. apart under a tent.

The plants are then grown on under the cloches until April – say the second or third week – when they can be planted into specially prepared beds as described in rows 1 ft apart and 9 in. between the plants.

If you don't want to transplant, the seed should be sown in February or March in rows 1 ft apart, with the drills ½ in. deep. The cloches should be put into position a fortnight before, to make sure that the soil is warm; the seed should be sown thinly. Some prefer to sow three seeds at 6 in. intervals along the rows and to thin the seedlings down to one if the three grow. The cloches should then be left in position until the leaves start to touch the glass, when they may be removed, to be replaced by taller cloches or because the cloches are needed for other crops.

GENERAL NOTES   Onions should never be transplanted deeply, for if they are they tend to grow like leeks. Any hoeing that is done should be away from the plants rather than up to them.

Care should be taken when transplanting in the open to prevent damage by onion fly, and whizzed or flaked naphthalene should be used as a preventative.

HARVESTING   The bulbs should ripen naturally in September, but to help them the tops are usually bent over at the neck. It is than that Access frames or cloches may be put over – they help considerably in the ripening-off process. A few weeks later it should be possible to pull the onions up and lay them on their sides, still under cloches, when the bottoms will dry off properly.

VARIETIES
Autumn sowing:
Salad

| The Queen | To be grown where White Lisbon has proved subject to disease. |
| White Lisbon | The favourite variety for pulling green. |

Summer bulbing

| Primodoro | A long-keeping onion of good size. |
| Unwin's Reliance | One of the heaviest-cropping varieties. |

Spring sowing:
January for planting out

| Selected Ailsa Craig | Produces very large, heavy bulbs. |
| The Premier | A huge onion of exhibition type. |

February – March sowing *in situ*

| Bedfordshire Champion | Good bulbs of mild flavour. |
| Rijnsburger Robusta | A new variety – an excellent keeper. |

Celery

Celery growing may be divided into two main groups: (a) celery grown in trenches, and (b) celery grown on top of the ground, which almost bleaches itself.

To get the best results it is always necessary to sow celery seed under glass. Most people raise plants by sowing in a greenhouse in January or February. The sowing is done in boxes, the seedlings being transplanted into further boxes, then into frames and finally into their permanent position.

By raising celery plants under cloches, time and effort are saved, and hardier and better plants result. Cloches are *not* used throughout the growth of the plants, though this is possible with self-bleaching celery if the taller barn cloches are available.

Celery propagated under Access frames

SOWING THE SEED   Buy seed that is guaranteed free from the spores of phoma root rot and septoria blight. Sow the seed in the shallowest of drills, 4–6 in. apart, sprinkling it so that it falls about ⅛ in. apart. Whiten the seeds first with lime, to make them visible. Rake the soil over lightly and cover with cloches, being sure to seal up the ends of the row with sheets of glass. The rows should be 5 in. apart under the cloches.

The sowing should be done in Mid-February or early March on soil that has been enriched with sedge peat lightly raked in at, say, half a bucketful to the square yard.

THINNING AND TRANSPLANTING   Thin the seedlings out to 6 in. apart when they have developed three or four leaves, and transplant the thinnings to 4 in. square under further cloches. Again see that there is plenty of organic matter in the top 6 in. of soil by forking in horticultural peat or similar material at half a bucketful to the square yard. As a result the plants will be properly developed and of a good size by the beginning of June, when they should be transferred to their permanent quarters in trenches 9 in. apart.

FROST PROTECTION   Large cloches can be used once more to cover the rows early in the winter, when frost and rain may threaten to spoil the crop. Cloche-covered rows of celery keep going until the middle of March.

American Green	Does not need blanching.
Giant Prize Pink	Excellent quality, keeps well.
Giant Red	Solid sticks of good size.
Giant White	Produces solid, firm sticks, crisp, and of good flavour.

Self-bleaching celery

Crops of self-bleaching celery keep going until the middle of November. This is an interesting crop for the cloche user, for it saves him digging trenches and he has celery much earlier in the year.

SOWING THE SEED   As for ordinary celery.

THINNING AND TRANSPLANTING   As for ordinary celery.

PLANTING OUT   The soil used for planting out should be enriched with plenty of properly composted organic refuse. In addition, a good fish manure, a meat and bone meal or a good organic fertilizer should be lightly forked in at 5–6 oz per square yard.

The plants should be set out in rows either 9 in. or 1 ft apart, depending on the cloches to be used, and 1 ft apart in the rows in either case. The ground should be well soaked with water before planting, and during the season it will be necessary to give thorough soakings with water once a week or so when the weather is dry. Little drills may be drawn out on either side of the rows of continuous cloches to act as water conduits.

BLEACHING   In order to help self-bleaching celery to bleach properly, it is a good plan to use large cloches to cover, say, a row at a time. The insides of the cloches should be whitewashed, as well as the sheet at the end of each row used to close up the ends; squares of asbestos can be used instead. It usually takes about 14 days for the plants to become fully white.

HARVESTING   This can be done directly the celery is sufficiently bleached.

VARIETIES
Dore	The best pure white dwarf, good flavour.
Golden Self-Blanching	Very solid, blanches easily.

Leeks

As the severest of winters cannot harm leeks, cloches are used solely for raising the plants. They are a valuable vegetable, for they can be used in the winter when other vegetables are scarce, and may be dug up as and when required.

SOWING THE SEED   This should be done in January, February, or early March, as advised for onions. The earlier the sowing, naturally the earlier the crop, and for the sake of continuity it is a good plan to make three small sowings under continuous cloches, say on 5 January, 5 February and 5 March.

Thin and shallow sowing is important, as in the case of onions, and plenty of finely divided organic matter, such as de-acidified peat, should be forked into the top 3 or 4 in., so that a good root system can be formed early in the plant's life.

TRANSPLANTING   The tent cloches can be left in position over the leeks until the leaves reach the top. Then they can be transplanted into their permanent quarters, about 1 ft between the rows and 8 in. apart in the rows.

To get the best plants it is advisable to thin out the seedlings in their early stages and transplant under further cloches, again as advised for onions.

VARIETIES

Empire	A medium variety, very suitable for the north.
Giant Musselburgh	Long thick white stems, popular in Midlands.
Marble Pillar	Produces an enormous stem, one of the best flavoured.
The Lyon	Good thick white stems, delicious flavour.
Walton Mammoth	An early variety, mild, agreeable flavour.

Shallots

Shallots are one of the easiest vegetables to grow, and they are quite hardy. Some people, however, like to cover them with cloches after planting, for then they are never disturbed by birds and, because of the extra warmth given by the cloches, they start earlier, giving heavier yields as a result. The cloches should only be left in position for a month or 6 weeks.

PLANTING   Planting should be done so that the rows are about
1 ft apart and the bulbs spaced out 4 in. apart in the rows. Quite
a good place to plant shallots is along the tops of celery trenches,
or to form an edging to a path.

RIPENING   Shallots can be helped to ripen properly if cloches
are put over the top when the leaves start to turn yellow. You
must not close the ends in this case, as you want the air to
circulate.

VARIETIES

The Russian shallot (sometimes called the Dutch or Jersey shallot)	Produces a large, round bulb.
The true (red or yellow) shallot	Does not produce as large a bulb as the above variety, but gives a nice firm bulb of the right size for pickling. Keeps well.

Spinach
There are two types of spinach: winter spinach, which has
prickly seeds, and summer spinach, which has round seeds. The
winter spinach usually is sown to live through the autumn, and
the summer spinach sown in the spring. Under cloches, however, it is a good plan to sow the prickly-seeded type all the year
round.

It is possible, under cloches, to have spinach in use 6 weeks
before normal sowings are possible outside.

SOILS AND MANURES   Spinach will grow on almost any soil.
When preparing the ground, good powdery compost should be
forked in 2–3 in. down, at the rate of one good barrowload to 10
square yard. In addition, meat and bone meal, hoof and horn
meal, a good fish manure or any of the proprietary organic
fertilizers should be forked in at 4 oz to the square yard.

SOWING THE SEED   Under the cloches this may be done at almost
any time of the year. Winter sowings are particularly successful.
It is a good plan to make a sowing once a month from October
until February, for it is usually during the winter and very early
spring that greens are scarce.

Aim at having the drills 1 ft apart and 1 in. deep. Sow the seed
very thinly and, directly the seedlings are large enough to be

handled, thin to 6 in. apart, transplanting the thinnings under further cloches if necessary.

In the case of very wet soil it is advisable to sow the seed on raised beds. These may be, say, 5 ft wide and 3 in. above the level of the surrounding soil. It is quite possible to have the rows as close as 8 in. apart if this makes it convenient to fit them under the size of cloches available.

GENERAL NOTES   If you are going to use cloches for spinach in the summer you will find that you have to give regular floodings to prevent the spinach from going to seed. Cloches, however, are better used for other crops during hot weather.

Winter spinach should not be picked too hard, the largest leaves being taken each time. In the case of summer spinach under cloches, it is better to pull up the whole plant when ready, and use it.

VARIETIES

Broad Leaved Prickly	Hardy, crops heavily.
Monarch Long Standing	Prickly-seeded, long-standing, large-leaved.

Spinach beet

This is a perpetual spinach which may be started under cloches. The seed should be sown late in March, though it is possible to make another sowing out of doors in August. The rows should be 15 in. apart and the plants thinned out to this distance.

A month or 6 weeks after seed-sowing it should be possible to remove the cloches and use them for other crops.

Seakale spinach

The stems are wide and ivory-white and used as seakale, while the leaves at the top are used as spinach. It is a biennial-type crop, and goes on producing both leaves and stems for months at a time.

SOILS AND MANURES   As for beetroot.

SOWING THE SEED   The rows should be 18 in. apart and the plants should be thinned to 15 in. apart in the rows.

GENERAL NOTES   Cloches are used, if necessary, to start the crop off well. The plants then go on cropping through the cold, wet periods.

New Zealand Spinach

New Zealand spinach is an invaluable summer vegetable which should be more widely grown. It goes on cropping until well on in October and never seems affected by even the hottest weather. Normally, plants have to be raised under glass and put out late in May, for New Zealand spinach is susceptible to frost.

SOWING THE SEED   It is possible to sow seed under cloches in April where the plants are to grow. The drills should be 1 in. deep, and the seed should be spaced out 4 in. apart.

TRANSPLANTING   Directly the spinach is large enough to handle it should be transplanted into rows 3 ft apart, leaving 2 ft between the plants. Cloche covering will again be necessary, and it is sometimes convenient to cover each plant individually with a four-sided cloche for this purpose. New Zealand spinach plants transplant better if the original soil in which they are sown has plenty of finely divided organic matter, such as sedge peat, incorporated into the top 3 in.

Another method is to sink 3-in. pots up to their rims in the ground, as close to one another as possible, fill them with Alex No-Soil compost, and sow one seed in each. The plants can then be left in the pots for 6 weeks or more, when they can be transplanted into the open.

GENERAL NOTES   When the plants creep along the ground and spread out too wide for the cloches, these should be removed and used for other crops. Keep the ground hoed between the plants as long as possible, and when the weather is dry soak with water.

Vegetable marrows

SOILS AND MANURES   Marrows are commonly grown on heaps, either made up specially for the purpose or ordinary rubbish heaps. Actually they do well in any soil, provided it is heavily manured. With clay soil and in wet years they prefer growing on a slight mound – as a result, their roots will be drier; but with light soils and in dry years they do best on the flat.

As much organic material as possible should be forked into the soil where the marrows are to grow. It is a good plan to make furrows 9 in. deep and to half-fill these with well-decayed manure or compost. This should then be trodden down and the soil replaced, thus forming a ridge over the manure. A certain amount of bottom heat is generated, and the plants get away quickly in consequence. In addition to the organic manure used, a complete organic fertilizer should be forked into the top 2 or 3 in. at 3–4 oz to the square yard.

SOWING THE SEED   The seeds may either be sown under lantern cloches where the plants are to grow, or in pots sunk into the ground to rim level, side by side under a row of continuous cloches. The pots should be filled with a mixture consisting of 2 parts soil, 1 part sedge peat and 1 part coarse silver sand, adding to each 3-gallon bucketful of this mixture 1½ oz of bone meal and 1 oz of ground limestone or chalk.

One seed should be sown ½ in. deep in the centre of each pot, and having plunged the pots into the centre of the rows close together up to their rims, they should be covered with large tent or low barn cloches, closing the ends with sheets of glass.

The seeds should be sown about the second week of April, and if there is any danger of frost at night, the cloches should be covered with old sacks or hessian. It will be necessary to water the pots from time to time, but the plants can grow on in their pots, under the cloches, until the characteristic leaves have developed. Planting out is done after all fear of frost is past – say about the third week of May.

It is possible, of course, to sow the seed *in situ*, i.e. where the plants are to grow, at the end of March in warm districts and in mid-April in the colder parts. Bush varieties sown 3 ft apart are the best. The centre part of each planting position (where the seed is to be sown) should be slightly higher than the rest of the ground.

TRANSPLANTING   If you want to go on growing the marrows under large cloches, the plants should be put out in rows 3 ft apart, with 3 ft between the plants. Each plant will have its own large barn cloche covering it, the ends being closed with sheets of glass. The cloche is then left in position until the plant fills it completely, the end-pieces of glass being removed some time in June.

When growing trailing marrows to climb up fences, pergolas or wire netting, the plants should be 4 ft apart, and should be put in 1 ft away from the fence or post. A special hole can be prepared for each one, a spade's depth and a spade's width, burying a forkful of compost at the bottom of each. The plants are then put into position and covered with large lantern-type cloche, which are removed when the trailers start to grow.

VARIETIES On the flat the bush-type marrows should be grown. Two good varieties are Bush-shaped Green and Bush-shaped White. For climbing Long Green is to be recommended, and so is the white trailing type known as Clucas' Roller.

White Custard	Most attractive shape with fluted edge.
Zephyr	Pale green fruits flecked with grey, almost cylindrical.
Zucchini	Very suitable for cloche work, fruits can be cut as courgettes.

Potatoes

Cloches can be used for raising particularly early potatoes.

SOILS AND MANURES The ideal soil is a deep, well-drained loam, neither too heavy nor too light. The land should be prepared by deep working, the organic manure used being placed into the drills at planting time. It is pointless to apply artificial manures on very early potatoes, for the tubers are out of the ground before they can make use of this extra plant food.

TUBERS Certified Scotch or Irish seed should be used, about the size of a hen's egg. This should be obtained in December or early January, and the tubers should be placed in trays or shallow boxes in an airy, frostproof shed with plenty of light. A greenhouse is excellent for this purpose.

Shoots, sprouts or sprits should then develop, and by the second week of February these should be ½–1 in. long. Only two shoots should be allowed on each potato at planting time.

PLANTING Planting should be carried out at the end of the second week of February. The ground should be levelled a week beforehand, and large cloches should be put in rows in position where the potatoes are to be planted.

At the end of the week the cloches should be removed and a drill 2 in. deep drawn out. The potatoes should be planted 1 ft apart; place over the tubers a 3-in. deep layer of powdery brown compost. The ridge of compost will now be 2 in. high right down the row. Put the cloches into position and close the ends with sheets of glass kept in position by a strong wire or narrow post.

GENERAL NOTES   Tent cloches may be used to start with but, as the potatoes grow, these should be removed and taller cloches substituted. During the changeover, which is usually done when the plants are 6 or 7 in. high, earthing up may take place. The soil should be drawn 3 or 4 in. up the plants.

HARVESTING   The potatoes may be dug about the middle of May, starting at one end of the row and gradually working to the other end. The sheet of glass at the end of the row should be replaced each time.

INTERCROPS   Radishes or lettuces may be grown on either side of the rows as an intercrop, provided they are cut before they are fully hearted.

VARIETIES   It is essential to choose a variety which is early and does not make too much haulm. Suttons Foremost and Ulster Chieftain are recommended.

10 Salad plants

Continuous cloches are ideal for all salad crops, for underneath them the plants grow naturally, and yet receive no check.

Endive
This is a salad plant which is much used on the Continent and is becoming increasingly popular in England.

SOILS AND MANURES   Almost any soil will grow endive well, provided it is rich in organic matter. Grow this crop, therefore, on land that has been previously well treated with compost and, if this is impossible, fork in composted vegetable refuse, burying it 3 or 4 in. down. In addition, into the top 1–2 in. rake fish manure, meat and bone meal, hoof and horn meal or any other good complete organic fertilizer. Use either of these at 4 oz to the square yard.

SOWING THE SEED   Rake the soil down level and work it into fine particles. A week or 10 days before the seeds are to be sown, place the cloches or frames in position to warm the soil. Draw out drills about ¾ in. deep and 1 ft apart. Sow the seeds in threes 12 in. apart along the drills, thinning the seedlings down to one if all three grow. These extra seedlings may be transplanted if necessary, but the best hearts are obtained if the seeds are sown where the plants are to grow.

After sowing, rake down level again and cover with cloches or frames, closing up the ends of the cloche rows with a sheet of glass.

For a continuous supply, four main sowings are possible: (1) mid-June, (2) mid-July, (3) mid-August and (4) mid-September.

BLEACHING   When the plants are fully grown they should be bleached before being used. This is best done by removing the cloches or frames and coating the insides thickly with whitewash before putting them back into position again. The sheet of glasss at the ends of each row should be treated in a similar manner.

If you don't want to whitewash the panes, it is possible to remove them and to put in similar-sized squares of asbestos sheet; these are excellent for bleaching the endive, and the glass can be put back again afterwards. It takes a long time to wash off the whitewash, and so many gardeners prefer to use asbestos; some have a special reserve of asbestos cloches for using during the winter months.

GENERAL NOTES   If the weather is dry, draw out drills on either side of the cloche rows, filling them up with water from time to time. Do not water during the week before bleaching.

VARIETIES

Golda	Taller plants with broad erect leaves.
Green Batavian	Leaves more like a lettuce, the most popular kind in Britain.
Moss-curled	Leaves crinkly and crisp.

Corn Salad

Corn salad is sometimes known as Lamb's lettuce. It is a much neglected salad crop and which is very useful from Christmas onwards.

SOILS AND MANURES   The ground should be prepared as for endive.

SOWING THE SEED   The seed should be sown at three periods — mid-June, mid-July and mid-September; continuity throughout the winter is then assured.

The rows should be 8 in. apart, the drills ½ in. deep and the seedlings thinned to 8 in. apart in the drills.

Although seed-sowing may be carried out in the open, the highest germination rate results when the rows are covered with cloches or frames.

GENERAL NOTES   The leaves of corn salad resemble the forget-me-not; they may either be gathered one at a time or whole plants may be pulled up and used at once. The cloche covering is best done from late October onwards; the great advantage is that the plants are kept clean.

VARIETIES

Broad-leaved	Dark, very delicious.
Regence	Has more pointed leaves.

Lettuce

Lettuces are undoubtedly one of the best crops for growing under cloches. They enable the gardener to produce plants with beautiful hearts almost all the year round. Plants grown under cloches are ready 3 weeks or a month sooner than similar sowings made in the open. Naturally, to get these results it is necessary to choose a sunny place for the early spring and autumn crops, so that the plants can obtain the maximum sunshine for that time of the year.

SOILS AND MANURES   You cannot expect to produce first-class lettuces unless your soil is well cultivated and generously manured. The land should therefore be forked, and brown powdery composted vegetable waste added at the rate of one good bucketful to the square yard. In addition, sedge peat should be worked into the top 2 in. at the rate of half a 2-gallon bucketful to the square yard. If the soil is dry, this peat should be damped thoroughly first of all. At the same time, incorporate a good organic fertilizer, such as fish manure or meat and bone meal, at the rate of a good handful to the square yard.

Rake the surface level, remove all the large stones and bits of debris, and put the cloches into position, sealing the ends of the rows with sheets of glass. Put the cloches into position to warm up the soil a week or more before sowing or transplanting.

SOWING THE SEED   It is most important to sow the right varieties at the right time. Some kinds are best adapted to the spring period, when the days are short. Others only thrive in the long, sunny days of summer. Never sow lettuce seed deeper than about ¼ in.; it saves a tremendous amount of thinning to sow two or three seeds at stations the right distance apart, rather than to sow in a complete row.

There are six main sowings:

Sowing no. 1. The first sowing should be made early in January or, in the north of England, about mid-February. The rows should be 7 or 8 in. apart, the outside ones being approximately 4 in. away from the glass sides of the cloches when these are in position. Naturally the number of rows will depend on the width of the cloche. Immediately after sowing draw a small amount of the soil into the drill with an iron rake used upside down, so as to cover the seed. Put the cloches back into position and close the ends of the rows with sheets of glass.

Late in February or early in March the lettuce seedlings will need thinning. If you have sown in stations, your object will be to thin down to one plant per station, but if you have sown in a continuous row, you must thin out to 2 in. apart, and then, three weeks later, to 4 in. apart. A fortnight after that, thin to 8 in. apart. The plants that remain will then develop rapidly, and produce good hearts for use in May.

Pricking out lettuces into a frame

The seedlings of the first and second thinnings can be transplanted under other cloches, and will provide good hearts later in May or early in June. The little plants from the last thinning should not be transplanted, but used in salad.

The best varieties for these first sowings are Minetto, Hilde and Kloek.

Sowing no. 2. The second sowing should take place during the third week of March in the same way as the first sowing, except that at thinning time it is necessary to put the plants 10 to 12 in. apart, for they tend to grow larger. The thinnings from this sowing do not transplant well, and if they *have* to be moved choose a dull, damp day and a piece of ground that contains plenty of moisture-holding material.

This crop does not need the protection of cloches after the middle of May. They may therefore be removed and used for another crop. Good varieties for this sowing are Improved Trocadero and Webb's Wonderful. The latter is known as an iceberg lettuce, and produces thicker, crisper, curlier leaves than most varieties. It is particularly delicious.

Sowing no. 3. It is most important with this sowing to see that there is plenty of fine organic matter in the soil. It is even worthwhile forking in a bucketful of damp medium-grade sedge peat to the square yard, because the lettuces will have to withstand drought conditions in the summer. Many gardeners water the seed beds thoroughly 2 days before sowing, so that the water goes down 4 in.

This sowing is made during the middle of May, and can be done without cloches. The best varieties are All-the-Year-Round and Continuity.

Sowing no. 4. This sowing is made in the open, but in such a way that cloches can be used to cover the crops at the end of September. Gardeners often make two sowings at this period, one on about 10 August and the other on about 20 August. The lettuces that result are cut in October and November.

Good varieties for this sowing are Unrivalled and Feltham King.

Sowing no. 5. This is regarded by most cloche or frame users as the most important sowing of all. It should produce beautiful, firmhearted specimens to cut during the whole of April and early May. Prepare the ground thoroughly, and place the cloches in position at the beginning of October. Sow the seed about 14 October, though in the north it may be advisable to sow a week or two before this. Sow thinly, and when the two

Lifting a box of lettuce out of an Access frame

seed leaves have fully developed the seedlings should be thinned to 4 in. apart. Please note the importance of thinning as early as this. These baby seedlings with only two leaves may be transplanted under other cloches so that the foliage is above the surface soil. During January a further thinning is done to 8 in. apart, and the second thinnings also may be transplanted under other cloches to 8 in. apart.

The best varieties for this sowing are Unrivalled and Amanda.

Sowing no. 6. In the midlands and the south it is usual to sow seeds under cloches in late October or early November, and then to transplant the seedlings as soon as the seed leaves are fully developed, 3 in. apart each way under further cloches. Here the little plants grow on until March, when they are planted out into the open and produce good heads in May or June.

The best varieties for this purpose are Imperial Winter and Amanda.

GENERAL NOTES   Though six main sowing periods have been given, it is possible to sow a pinch of seed regularly every 10 days from early March until the end of July.

Cos lettuce may be grown under cloches as a spring crop, and do best planted in the centre of a large cloche row with a row of the cabbage type on either side. They may be sown under cloches in the autumn, and the plants from such sowings are then put out into the open ground in March.

The best cos varieties are Balloon and Paris White.

Radishes

Radishes can be grown under cloches as a catch-crop, as an intercrop, or as a crop on their own at almost any time of the year. The results are particularly valuable when sowings are made under cloches or frames during January, February, March and early April. Cloche-grown radishes are crisp and hard, and never fibrous and 'hot'.

SOILS AND MANURES   Any soil will do, preferably one on the light side. No special manuring is necessary. It is advisable, however, to see that there is plenty of organic matter, such as sedge peat, in the top 3 or 4 in., so the soil may be treated as advised for endive.

SOWING THE SEED   Sow the seeds shallowly and very thinly as they need to be ½ in. apart. Water the drills if the weather is dry. Cover the ground with cloches for at least a week before sowing, and again immediately after sowing, and firm, succulent roots will be produced.

GENERAL NOTES   Sowings may be made in shallow drills between the rows of lettuces or on both sides of a single row. They may also be made in the same drill as lettuce, carrot or onion seed, etc., the radishes being pulled early.

VARIETIES
Cherry Belle	Scarlet, glove-shaped.
French Breakfast	Perhaps the most delicious.
Inca	Turns in quickly, resistant to sponginess.
Scarlet Globe	A lovely crimson colour.

Mustard and cress
There is no difficulty at all in growing mustard and cress under cloches or frames at almost any time of the year except January and February. The soil should be well enriched with finely divided organic matter such as sedge peat, as advised for endive. The seed should be sown on the surface of the ground after it has been got down to a fine tilth or, if preferred, on damp sacking laid on the ground for this purpose. This ensures that the salad keeps free from grit. A good soaking with water should then be given if the weather is dry, the cloches being put into position immediately afterwards and the ends of the short rows closed with a sheet of glass. Cut with scissors – do not pull up. Sow cress 3 days before mustard so that they are ready simultaneously.

Cucumbers
Growing cucumbers under cloches can be divided roughly into (a) the production of the ridge varieties and (b) and the production of frame varieties.
   The ridge types are started off under cloches, and go on growing in the open afterwards. Frame cucumbers have to be grown under cloches the whole time. Other than this, the preparation of the soil is very similar. Frame varieites are normally sown under glass and planted out; ridge varieties are generally sown *in situ*. Frame varieties go bitter if they are pollinated, and

so the male blossoms have to be removed; with ridge varieties this does not matter.

SOILS AND MANURES   Prepare the ground as advised for melons in Chapter 14. Cucumbers demand rich conditions as far as organic matter is concerned.

SOWING THE SEED   Seed sowing may be done in three ways:
1. In 3-in. pots (either peat or earthenware) sunk to the rims in the soil outside and covered with a large cloche made into a hand-light by closing the ends with a sheet of glass.
2. Three in. apart and ½ in. deep in a properly prepared seed bed under cloches for transplanting later.
3. At permanent stations where the plant is intended to grow (the best method of all).

In the last case the seed is sown in the centre of the mound by making a slight depression like a saucer and sowing the seed as soon as the temperature of the ground is 60 degrees F. This will usually be about the middle of April in the south, and the end of April in the midlands and the beginning of May in the north. By putting the cloches into position 7–10 days beforehand, the soil will be warmed. The butt of a pencil makes a nicely shaped hole, and it is usual to sow three seeds 1 in. apart under each cloche at planting position. If an upturned glass jam jar is used, two seeds may do, and the jam jar will be replaced by a larger cloche as soon as the growth of the plants makes it necessary.

PLANTING OUT   Where plants are raised in the greenhouse or under cloches or frames, it is usual to transplant the seedlings to the places where they are to grow directly they have made their first pair of true leaves. Here they will usually be placed 3 ft apart. Ridge varieties should be kept covered until they fill the cloches. Frame varieties are usually kept permanently covered and trained along a horizontal wire stretched tightly just underneath the head of the cloches or frames.

STOPPING AND POLLINATION   There is no need to stop ridge varieties after the first stopping at the seventh leaf, and all that needs to be done to the frame types is to stop them at one leaf beyond the forming cucumber. A lateral will then form, and this, in its turn, is stopped at one leaf beyond the cucumber, and so on. These laterals are usually tied to the wires as the work proceeds. It is possible, however, to allow both types of cucumber to grow at will.

Pinch off the male blooms from the frame varieties to prevent them pollinating the female blossoms, which makes the cucumbers bitter. The male flowers, however, are needed on ridge varieties, and should not be removed.

VENTILATION AND FEEDING   Ridge varieties will, of course, need no special ventilation, as the cloches will be removed some time early in June. In the case of frame cucumbers, treat them as for melons (see Chapter 14).

Feed as advised for melons, using a liquid manure.

HARVESTING   Cut the cucumbers as desired. Never let them become too old. Keep cutting, therefore, when they are a good size, and the plants will keep cropping. It is possible to get 40 good cucumbers from a ridge variety, and about half that number from a good frame type.

VARIETIES

Burpee Hybrid	Best of all ridge types, large cucumbers, plants crop heavily, fruits almost spineless.
Conqueror	The best of frame varieties for continuous cloche work.
Perfection King of the Ridge ⎫ Victory ⎭	Two good ridge varieties, but neither as large as Burpee.
Telegraph Improved	Use this variety when it is impossible to get Conqueror.

NB The ridge varieties are easy to grow and should be tried by the beginner. The frame varieties are more popular and have a better flavour on the whole and so should be grown after some experience.

11 Tomatoes

One of the great advantages of using cloches or Access frames for tomato growing is that (a) the plants can be put out much earlier and (b) they can be protected from the frost in the autumn and so all the fruits that develop can be made to ripen properly. It enables the northern gardener to grow tomatoes in the open just as easily as gardeners in the south. The cloche or frame grower does not share the difficulties encountered by the greenhouse grower, because the former can rotate his tomatoes and this means that he has them in one part of the garden one year and in another part the next, and thus his soil never becomes 'tomato-sick'.

Hygiene
When raising tomatoes, attention must be paid to hygiene and smokers must be careful to wash their hands in strong disinfectant, for the viruses which infect tobacco plants are never killed during the curing, and these can be transmitted. In addition, of course, the pots and boxes should be quite clean, and it is good idea to dip them for 48 hours in a tank containing a solution of green Rentokil.

Compost under cloches
When tomatoes are sown in pots in the greenhouse Alex No-Soil compost should be used and it is a good idea for the soil under the cloches to be treated in a similar way. Appropriate proportions of fine sedge peat and sand should be mixed into the top 4 in. of soil together with the necessary plant foods. Another method is to remove the top 2 or 3 in. of soil and replace this with the Alex compost mixture. It is always worthwhile taking the utmost trouble in preparing the soil for seed growing.

Dates of sowing
These will, of course, conform to the dates that the plants are required for putting out in the garden, and the sample table below gives some guidance:

Cloche-raised plants

Variety	Date sown	Date transplanted	Date de-cloched	Date of first pick
Outdoor	27 March	10 June	28 June	28 July
Open air	31 March	15 June	29 June	24 August

Sowing the seeds

It has been made clear above that the soil under the cloches should be made as similar to the Good Gardeners' Association compost as possible, the formula for this being 2 parts by bulk of good soil, 1 part of sedge peat and 1 part of coarse silver sand. To this compost is added 1½ oz of bone meal and ¾ oz of ground chalk per bushel (a bushel of soil goes exactly in a box 22 in. long, 10 in. wide and 10 in. deep).

The method, therefore, is to add the sedge peat, sand, bone meal and lime, and then to fork this along the strip to be covered by the cloches. In cases where the soil has been used again and again for cloche crops it is worthwhile making up the compost above and using it as a top dressing 1 in. deep. Incidentally, the bone meal and lime are usually added at 3 oz to the yard run, the peat at a bucketful to the yard run and the coarse sand at a similar rate. If the soil is heavy but the land very sandy, the coarse sand dressing may be omitted.

Some gardeners always remove the top few inches of soil which is going to be exactly under the cloches and replace it with the compost described above. This takes longer but the soil mixture, as a result, is perfect. In both cases, the seeds should be sown 1½ in. square and ¼ in. deep. Shade the cloches by throwing a few sacks here and there after sowing until the seedlings are well developed, and either transplant the seedlings to their permanent positions from where they are growing by getting them up carefully with a trowel, or pot them up into peat pots when they are 3 in. high, or into home-made 'soil blocks'. Put the potted plants into a trench 3 in. deep, cut to the appropriate width and length so that the cloches can be placed over the top to cover the plants.

Watering may have to be done from time to time but it will be found that plants under cloches never dry out as quickly as they do in the greenhouse.

General notes

1. Always handle the seedlings with clean hands and never squeeze the stems in any way.

2. Never transplant during cold, windy weather.
3. Always use reliable, healthy seed.
4. Be ready to give protection during excessive frost or sunshine during the earlier part of the season.
5. Tend to underwater rather than overwater.
6. Look out for the rogues known as feather-heads or Christmas trees. These plants have a dwarf, leafy appearance with more side shoots. They must be destroyed in the early stages.
7. Don't handle the plants with nicotine stains on your fingers.

The site

This should be where the plants are sheltered from north and east winds – a south border is best or one with a wall or strong fence at the back. These borders are usually very dry, so make sure that they are thoroughly flooded during digging and that there is plenty of humus in the top 3–4 in.

Preparation of soil and site

Any properly prepared soil will grow tomatoes, although heavy clay will need to be covered with compost in the autumn, which should be raked into the soil in the spring. Light soils need plenty of properly composted vegetable matter. Fork this in about 2 or 3 in. and in addition apply sedge peat, which should be soaked well first. Light soils are likely to be lacking in potash, and so wood ashes should be applied at ½ lb to the square yard.

When preparing the soil be sure to pick out any perennial weed roots, and remove the little shining globular eggs of slugs if you see them. Apply hydrated lime at the rate of 5–6 oz to the square yard when the tomatoes are to be planted on the flat. When planting in a trench, fork the soil over and leave it rough; incorporate the compost into it a fortnight before planting.

Don't forget in either case to use sedge peat at half a bucketful to the square yard and a complete organic fertilizer like hoof and horn meal to which potash has been added at 4–5 oz to the square yard. These ingredients are raked into the top 1–2 in. of soil either in the trench or on the flat, about 10 days before planting.

Trenches

Many gardeners have found that trench planting gives excellent results, because it gives the cloches extra height and therefore the plants can stay under them for a longer period. Dig out shallow trenches 6 in. deep and a spade's width, throwing the soil up evenly on either side – the width of the trench at the top should be at least 6 in. narrower than the spread of the cloches used. Dark brown powdery compost should be put in the trench so that when it is trodden down it is at least 2 in. thick. This should be raked into the bottom of the trench and well trodden down again, putting 3 in. of good soil or Alex No-Soil compost over the top.

The trench should now be about 4 in. below the normal soil level and should be covered with cloches; seal the ends of the cloche row with large sheets of glass. The tomatoes can be planted in 10 days' time.

Soil moisture

If the subsoil appears very dry when the land is forked over in the autumn, water it well. The flooding should be done after the organic matter has been forked in and before the Alex compost goes on top. Fill the trench with water once or twice and let it soak through, thus making certain that there is plenty of water below.

Choosing good plants

The best plants for raising under cloches are those that are sturdy, short-jointed and dark green, with not too many side shoots. Water the plants well the day before they are put out so that the leaves are firm and turgid. If they are in paper or peat pots the whole pot is planted and so there is no root disturbance. If they are in clay pots, put the plants and the pot into the hole for 2 or 3 days before knocking out, so that the temperature of the soil in the pot and the ground round about are approximately equal.

Planting

This should be done very firmly so that the lowest leaves are at soil level, making sure that the stem is never squeezed or pinched. Remove the crocks and insert your fingers at the bottom of the ball of soil to spread the roots out a little. Never press the soil around the stem itself but make sure that the ball of soil is really firm, leaving a little depression around the plant for watering afterwards – this is called ball-watering.

Staking

Method no. 1. A wire is stretched tightly between two stout stakes, one at each end of the trench and 2 in. below the top of the cloche. A short bamboo is inserted for each plant and tied firmly to the wire; the plant is trained up the stake and then bent carefully round and trained along the wire.

Method no. 2. One stake is pushed in vertically for each plant and another at an angle of about 45 degrees, and the tops of the stakes are tied together – these are arranged so that they are just below the ridge line of the cloches.

The side growth is tied to the vertical stake and the original main stem to the sloping one. The taller the cloches used and the longer the stakes the more trusses the plant can set, and the growing points of both stems must be pinched out when they reach the top if the plants are to remain under glass coverings throughout growth.

Method no. 3. This is very much the same as Method no. 1 except that a length of string is tied to the wire and very loosely to the bottom of the plants. The string should be slightly slack so that the plant can be twisted round it as it climbs.

Method no. 4. Get the plants growing well under the cloches, using either a short stake or none at all until the glass covering is removed. Then give each one a 5-ft bamboo or string and run a top wire along about 4 ft 6 in. from soil level.

Dis-shooting

Remove the side shoots which develop in the axils of the leaves as the plants grow – this usually has to be done once a week, at the same time removing any yellow leaves at the bottom of the plants. Cut the shoots out cleanly at their base with the tip of a sharp-bladed knife when they are just under 1 in. long. If you are going to adopt the double stem system, only one shoot should be left at the base of the plant.

Tying-in and defoliating

The plants should be tied to the stakes immediately above a leaf, wrapping the string once round the string or wire and then round the stem in a loop large enough to allow for expansion; this should be done about every 6 in. up the plant. Do not remove any of the leaves until the fruits begin to ripen unless (a) they are turning yellow or (b) the foliage is too thick and preventing the sun from ripening the tomatoes. To make certain that botrytis does not spread, rub the cut end with a piece of liver of sulphur.

Stopping

This consists of pinching out or cutting out the growing points of the plants. It is done when the growing point reaches the top of the cloches or, in the cases where the cloches have been removed, when the fifth truss has developed. This always encourages the production of plenty of side growths so that further dis-shooting is necessary 10–14 days after the stopping.

Feeding

Apply 1 oz approximately per plant of a good tomato fertilizer with an organic base immediately the bottom truss has set, and apply this in a ring round each plant as far as the foliage spreads, watering it in well. A liquid manure containing all the plant foods in their correct proportions may be used. A half-strength feed is applied after each flower truss sets, giving about ½ gallon of this liquid manure per plant. This feeding should stop after the top truss is ripening well, about a fortnight after the setting of this truss. Some gardeners prefer to apply organic liquid manure once a fortnight throughout the season at half strength.

If the plants appear to be growing too luxuriantly, they should be given an application of wood ashes at 6 oz to the yard run; good flue dust can be used instead at 4 oz to the yard run.

Mulching and filling up

Soaked sedge peat is very good for mulching the surface of the ground along the tomato rows, or in the bottom of the trench when the tomatoes are being grown in this way. This helps to keep the roots cool, and also the worms pull a great deal of this organic matter into the ground where it will feed the plants. Mulching should be done early in June and then covered early in July with a 2- or 3-in. depth of surface soil mixed with an equal proportion of peat to encourage the new set of young vigorous roots developing from the plants.

Fruit ripening

Plants which are stopped when they reach the top of the cloches will have their fruit ripened without being moved. However, if the cloches have been removed, the plants can be untied and laid down at the end of September and covered with cloches to assist ripening. First spread plenty of sedge peat or chopped-up wheat straw on the soil and allow the plants to rest on this, afterwards cutting away most of the foliage.

Wrapping

When the cloches are removed to allow the plants to grow naturally, they can be stood up on end side by side on the north side of the plants, or in a complete ring round each plant. This gives protection and also extra reflected heat to aid the ripening.

Extra height

A good way of giving extra height to the plants under the cloches is to draw up the soil on either side of the original trench and stand the cloches on this, or put boards or turves on either side on which the cloches can rest.

Another way of achieving added height is to place Access frames one on top of the other

Extra ventilation

The cloches can be stood apart so that there is a 1-in. space between them. If the sun is very hot in the south-west, these cloches should be sprayed with a little lime wash to prevent sun-scorch.

Pollination, sprinkling and watering

There is little trouble with pollination as the insects which do this work like to get under the cloches – they can always find a tiny crack by which to enter. Syringe the plants during the middle of the day with tepid water – this helps the pollen to germinate properly, and spraying the plants helps to distribute it. Do this work from either end of the rows with plenty of force.

Many blossoms drop off each year through dryness at the roots, so make sure that, when you water after the trusses have set, the plants are soaked. A good mulching after watering helps to conserve the moisture.

Picking
Gather the fruit when they are slightly unripe – when they are red but still firm. Lift them up carefully so that they come away from the 'spur' easily with the calyx on them and a short stalk. Do not on any account squeeze the fruit or they will bruise.

Tomatoes should be harvested when they are still slightly unripe

'Raising' the cloches

This is easily done by using what are called adaptor wires. An adaptor wire consists of a short wire rod, 23½ in. long, with a double hook at one end. Four adaptors are used for each cloche. The adaptors hold a wall of glass which supports the cloche perched on the top. As a rule, 12-in. glass is used, and the cloches are raised 11 in. For many crops, it is unnecessary to have glass below the cloches which are only required to keep off rain. In such cases, wire rectangles may be used instead of glass and they prove most satisfactory. Cloches raised in this way are reasonably rigid but must not be expected to stand up to gales.

VARIETIES

Grower's Pride	Early and vigorous, disease-resistant, very good cropper.
Histon Cropper	Compact plants but carrying very large crops of small to medium-sized fruit, slightly tart flavour.
Histon Early	A very heavy cropper, earlier than any existing tall variety, good sized, fine flavour.
Isabelle	Firm, round and fleshy fruit of excellent quality and flavour.
Sioux	An early cropper, producing perfectly shaped medium-sized fruit, flavour and quality good.

Tomatoes under Access frames

Cold grown tomatoes under these frames have an exquisite flavour and make an ideal summer crop. Bush tomatoes are best for the 1½–2 ft frame, and for this purpose the frames can be raised 6 in. on bricks or timber. Alternatively, the well-known greenhouse varieties can be grown in what is called the 'double decked' 4 × 4 ft frame. The idea is to place one frame on top of another and to hold them together by means of brackets supplied by the manufacturer.

Bush tomatoes should be planted out in mid-April, or even May in the north, i.e. when the weather gets warmer, and put the plants 2 ft apart each way. In the case of the 10 × 4 ft cloche, this means ten plants, while with the 4 × 4 ft only four plants fit in. Varieties such as Amateur, French Cross and Outdoor Girl are quite suitable for this purpose. It is advisable to limit the growth of the plants. This is best done by allowing a strong shoot in the top leaf axil to develop as well as four more strong shoots from the base of the plant. The intermediate shoots which emanate from the main stem are removed when they appear. Allow, say, three trusses on each of the five shoots. The shoots can be supported with twine attached to bamboo canes or wire, stretched tightly across the top of the arched legs of the frame.

'Amateur' bush tomatoes under Access frames

Give a liquid feed every 10 days once fruit has set. Maxicrop is good for this purpose, as is Seafood. Bush tomatoes have a good flavour and do very well in these frames. It is usual to get about 60 lb of tomatoes from the outdoor varieties. With greenhouse varieties, however, put four plants in the double decked 4 × 4 ft cloche – allow six to seven trusses per plant before it reaches the top of the frame, and then stop it by pinching out the growing part. Provide adequate support for the plants and train them in the usual way.

12 Herbs

Continuous cloches are invaluable in herb growing. They make it possible, for instance, to have fresh parsley all the year round, and they can force mint along so that it is ready for use a month earlier than from outside pickings.

Parsley

Seeds often germinate slowly when sown in the open. Some people regard parsley as a difficult crop to grow, but most problems disappear when continuous cloches are used.

SOILS AND MANURES   Parsley will grow on almost any soil, but heavy clays should be opened up by forking in sand, flue dust or other gritty material. Always give the surface of the ground a dressing of lime at 3–4 oz to the square yard before sowing the seed.

Fork in well-rotted organic matter 2 in. down, so that there is plenty of moisture-holding material. Rake into the top 1 in. a good organic fertilizer at 3 oz to the square yard.

SOWING THE SEED   Sow the seed *very* thinly, ½ in. deep. It makes a good edging plant. If you want several rows, have them 1 ft apart.

The best times for sowing are early March and early August. In the former case the cloches should be put into position a fortnight beforehand, to warm the soil. In the latter case the cloches may be put over immediately after sowing.

It is possible, too, to sow as late as September, if necessary and, in fact, almost every month during the summer, but if two good sowings are made as suggested there should be no difficulty in keeping up the supply all the year round.

THINNING   It is most important to thin early, before the plants get overcrowded. The thinning should be carried out to 6 in. apart.

Firm the ground well after thinning. It cannot be over-emphasized that parsley likes firm soil.

CUTTING DOWN   If the plants tend to get coarse they should be cut down, and the young growth which then comes up will be green and tender. Such hard cutting generally defers the flowering which does so much harm to the plants.

KEEPING THE ROW GOING   It is possible, by using cloches or frames, to keep a row of parsley going satisfactorily for 2 years. To do this it is necessary to cover the rows with cloches from November to early April.

Before covering at the beginning of November, part of the row may be cut down early in October, and this will provide plenty of young shoots in the spring. The rest of the row can just have some of the older leaves removed.

VARIETIES

Champion Moss-curled	Very dark green, tightly curled leaves.
Myatt's Garnishing	Long leaf-stalks, heavy cropper.

Mint

There are many kinds of mint available, the true spearmint being the most useful for mint sauce. It is, however, susceptible to mint rust. The variety rotundifolia is not so susceptible to rust, but some people dislike its hairiness.

SOILS AND MANURES   A damp situation seems to suit mint best. Almost any soil will do and any odd corner. A shady border is often used with success.

PLANTING   A mint bed should not remain down more than 2 years, and it is better to replant every year.

Naturally, if very early mint is required, a warm, sheltered position is advisable. Divide up the plants in March, and plant them out 6 in. apart in the rows, so that they can be covered with cloches when necessary.

In cases where rust is bad, wash the roots well before planting out, putting them afterwards in warm water at exactly 120 degrees F for 20 minutes.

SPECIAL FORCING   You can dig up mint roots early in November and, having washed them well, cut them up into portions not more than 1 in. long. These cut portions can then be planted thickly ½ in. deep in strips of sufficient width to be covered by the size of continuous cloches available.

Cutting up and covering with cloches, together with sealing the ends of the cloche rows with sheets of glass, cause quick growth, and mint may be produced a month or more earlier than by the normal way.

WINTER TREATMENT   Cut the stems down hard in November, putting the cloches into position. To provide additional warmth cover the bed with a layer of straw beforehand. Close up the ends of the cloches and excellent mint shoots will be ready to cut early in March.

Sage
Although it is possible to raise sage from seeds, it is always better to buy cuttings or plants. Plants raised from seed soon go to seed themselves.

SOILS AND MANURES   As advised for parsley.

CUTTINGS   These should consist of strong side shoots, which should be removed with a heel of old wood in April or May. There is no difficulty in rooting these cuttings in sandy soil, covered with continuous cloches. Shade the cloches until the cuttings have fully rooted.

PLANTING OUT   Plant out in rows 2 ft apart, with the plants 2 ft apart in the rows. Cover the cloches if necessary, removing them early in June. Cover again in mid-October.

REPLANTING   Aim at replanting sage rows every 4 years.

VARIETIES
Broad-leaved Green   The better type.
Red Sage   Has violet-coloured leaves, not very popular.

Thyme
Thyme is very useful for flavouring soups and stews.

PROPAGATION   It is always better to raise plants by division of roots in March and April, or by cuttings taken in September. You can raise plants by sowing seed but they are apt to flower too much, and then their flavour is not so good. Take cuttings in a similar manner to sage.

SOILS AND MANURES   As advised for parsley.

PLANTING   Thyme will form an effective edging to a border, and will grow in dry borders where parsley will not do so well.

Make the rows 2 ft apart, with the plants 18 in. apart in the rows. Replant every 3 or 4 years to prevent the plants becoming leggy.

COVERING   Put the cloches into position early in October, to give protection throughout the winter.

VARIETIES
Common Thyme   The usual variety.
Lemon Thyme   Has a more lemony flavour.

Chives
This is another plant that may be used as an edging to a border. It has a mild onion flavour. The shoots may be pulled almost all the year round.

SOILS   As advised for parsley.

PLANTING   Propagate by division early in the spring, and plant 8 in. apart. If there is more than one row, have them 1 ft apart.

COVERING   Cover about mid-September, to keep the chives going throughout the winter. If necessary, apply a little nitrate of soda along the rows early in the spring, to start them growing vigorously again. It is a good idea to cut down half the row of chives in July to ensure fresh growth, then the other half of the row in September.

13 More unusual vegetables

As a nation we are still very conservative about food, and there are many vegetables which are comparatively unknown, or which are thought too difficult to grow in the normal garden.

Asparagus, with which the chapter opens, is supposed to be the rich man's crop, but actually it is not difficult to grow, especially with the help of continuous cloches. It makes a pleasant change, too, in the early spring.

Asparagus

Cloches and Access frames are used with asparagus to encourage the plants to crop earlier. They cannot, of course, turn poor plants into strong, healthy ones. It is necessary, therefore, to follow the usual instructions for growing this crop.

SOILS AND MANURES   Asparagus may remain in the ground for 20 years, so it is well worthwhile spending some time on soil preparation. One barrowload of well-rotted powdery composted vegetable refuse should be incorporated into every 4 square yard. This forking should be done in the autumn.

Early in March, as soon as the ground is fit to work, rake the soil over, adding fish manure or some similar organic fertilizer at 4–5 oz per square yard. Finally dress the surface of the ground with hydrated lime at 4 oz to the square yard if the land is acid.

PLANTING   Although asparagus can be raised from seed, most people prefer to purchase plants to save time, for it is 4 years from the time of seed-sowing before you can take a crop.

Buy a good strain of asparagus such as Regal Pedigree. For covering with cloches, plant during the first 2 weeks of April, in ground that has been well prepared and is quite free from perennial weeds. Arrange the rows 3 ft apart. Choose showery weather if possible, and on no account expose the roots for a long period. Spread the roots out in spider fashion, and do not cover the crowns with more than 3 in. of soil.

GENERAL NOTES   Keep the beds free from weeds by hoeing and some hand weeding. During the summer give dried blood at 2 oz. to the square yard once every 2 months. Every spring give a dressing of bone meal at 4 oz to the square yard and sulphate of potash at 1 oz to the square yard.

Every autumn cover the beds with a 2-in. thickness of sedge peat or compost. Each January cover the bed with 1½ in. of soil. It is then that the organic fertilizers may be applied, and a week later the rows can be covered with continuous cloches.

HARVESTING   Do not cut sticks of asparagus the first year after planting, but every succeeding year after this cut the sticks as they appear, 3 in. below ground level, taking care not to damage the crowns of the plants. When plants are growing under cloches discontinue cutting about the middle of June.

As soon as the foliage turns yellow in the autumn, it should be cut down and burned.

VARIETIES

Connover's Colossal	Has slender, pointed buds, heavy cropper.
Early Argenteuil	An early variety bearing large, shapely, pointed buds, tinged with pink. An English selection of this type would appear to be Reading Giant.
Regal	The pedigree asparagus with the heaviest yields of large delicious sticks.

Chinese artichokes

This is a good crop to grow under cloches, for the plants appreciate the extra warmth. Pure white tubers are produced in abundance, and should be used from November to April, either in salads or cooked. The roots are delicious eaten raw, fried or boiled. The plant grows only 18 in. high, and so is quite suitable for the tent type of cloche.

SOILS AND MANURES   Choose a well-drained, free-working soil. Light soils should be improved by the addition of plenty of organic matter, while heavy soils should be lightened by the addition of sand or other inert material such as flue dust.

Before planting, fork into the ground a good fish manure or some other fertilizer with an organic base, at 4–5 oz to the square yard.

PLANTING   This should be done in April, in drills 6 in. deep. The rows should be 18 in. apart, and the tubers placed 9 in. apart in the rows. Choose an open, sunny situation.

GENERAL NOTES   Cover with cloches or frames immediately after planting. Leave the cloches in position until the end of June, when they may be used for some other crop if necessary.

HARVESTING   Lift the tubers about the third week of October and store in soil or sand in a shed, to prevent them from shrivelling. When lifting, all the roots that have formed should be removed. It is important to keep them covered to preserve their whiteness. They may be left in the ground if preferred, to be dug up when required.

Peppers
Capsicums are used for flavouring pickles, for putting into salads, or for cooking in soups or stews. They need plenty of water in the early stages.

SOILS AND MANURES   The soil may be prepared as for tomatoes, and manuring may be carried out in a similar manner.

SOWING THE SEED   The plants may be raised by sowing seeds under cloches as described for cucumbers.

PLANTING   The plants should be put out in their permanent positions 2 ft 3 in. apart, 15 in. apart in the rows. They may be grown under tall cloches or Access frames nearly the whole time, as they never grow as tall as tomatoes. The actual planting outside should be done about mid-May.

GENERAL NOTES   Capsicums will not as a rule stand moisture on the foliage. Watch out for red spider.

HARVESTING   Pick regularly as the fruits ripen. Gather the whole crop before the end of October. When you grow them without cloches you have to gather before the end of September.

CAPSICUMS AND AUBERGINES UNDER ACCESS FRAMES   Sow capsicum seed in heat in April, and that of aubergines in February – for temperature details, see melons (Chapter 14). Plant out the little plants in late May or early June. Incorporate dark brown powdery compost into the soil before planting, at one large bucketful to the yard run of cloche. Plant two rows 18 in. apart. Water regularly, preferably by irrigation; in fact, when the plants are touching, it is advisable to keep them thoroughly moist. During flowering time turn on the mist line for about 30 seconds every afternoon as this helps the fruits to set. Keep a check on red spiders which will be seen under the leaves. Spray the undersides of the foliage with liquid derris to control this pest.

Celeriac

Celeriac grows like a turnip, and yet tastes just like the delicious hard heart of celery. It is excellent when sliced in salads or when cooked. The vegetable will keep for 6 months after it is fully grown.

SOILS AND MANURES   As for beetroot.

PROPAGATION   As for celery.

PLANTING OUT   Planting may be done in May or early June in rows 18 in. apart, the plants being 12 in. apart in the rows.

GENERAL NOTES   Celeriac is a heavy feeder, so be prepared to give a liquid manure, such as Liquinure, from the end of June onwards, if possible once a week. Shallow drills may be drawn out on either side of the rows of cloches, and this liquid may be poured liberally down the drills to reach the roots.

The plants may be grown under continuous cloches from the beginning, and if tent cloches are used to start with, these should be replaced by taller barn cloches about mid-July.

HARVESTING   A fortnight before the hearts are to be lifted – say late October or earlier – the soil should be hoed well up to the foliage, to make the upper part of the root blanch. There is no need to put the cloches back again after this. Another method which has proved quite successful is to remove the cloches, whitewash the inside and replace them for a fortnight. The ends of the rows have to be closed, of course, to keep out the light. This blanching is not vital, but it ensures that the whole of the root is good.

The roots may be dug up and stored in soil in a shed, or in 'buries' or 'clamps' outside. In the south of England it is possible to leave them outside and use them as required, and in this case it is better to leave the continuous cloches over them.

Erfurt	Produces a smaller bulb of first-class quality.
Giant Prague	A good keeper, large, very solid.
Paris Ameliore	A good white variety, throws a large bulb.

Aubergine (egg plant)

Aubergine is a very delicious vegetable when cooked, and may be stuffed and baked, cut into slices and fried or even served boiled. It makes an excellent breakfast dish when fried.

SOILS AND MANURES   As for tomatoes.

SOWING THE SEED   As for tomatoes.

PLANTING   Plant under cloches as advised for tomatoes, in a sunny situation, a south border being very suitable. Arrange the plants 18 in. apart in 2 ft rows.

GENERAL NOTES   Grow the plants on a single stem from the beginning, and when they are strong enough pinch out the growing point to make them branch. Allow six shoots to form, and after this stop the side growths by pinching them.

Like capsicums, they are apt to be attacked by red spiders, so syringe them over with warm water occasionally in the evening, taking care to avoid damping off. Much of this can be done from the ends of the rows of cloches without removing them, but if the rows are long it may be necessary to removed occasional cloches to syringe underneath. If you have cloches with removable sides you should, of course, take them out.

From the end of July onwards the plants will grow in the open, especially in the south.

VARIETIES

Blanche Longue de la Chine	The long, white aubergine of delicious flavour, contains more 'meat' than the other varieties.
Noire de Pekin	Dark violet fruit, long.
Purple	Fine quality, large fruit, round, purplish.

Asparagus Peas

This is a very fascinating little pea to grow, and looks more like a vetch than an ordinary pea. It does not climb, but grows 18 in. high in a bushy form and bears masses of beautiful dark red blossoms which make it most attractive.

SOILS AND MANURES   As ordinary peas.

SOWING THE SEED   Sow the seeds under cloches in early March, where the plants are to grow. They grow quite well in a south border. If more than one row is needed the next should be 18 in. away. The seed is small, so the drills need be no deeper than ½ in.

Cover the ground, where the seeds are to be sown, with the continuous cloches a fortnight beforehand.

GENERAL NOTES   In dry weather water well in little drills drawn out on either side of the cloche rows.

HARVESTING   Pick regularly directly the pods are about 1½ in. long. If they are left on longer they get coarse. The pod is cooked as well; they are served whole and are very delicious.

Sweet corn

SOILS AND MANURES   Sweet corn will grow well on almost any type of soil, provided it is neither too heavy nor too light. It is probably best grown on land which has been well manured for a previous crop, for to dig in compost just before sowing sweet corn is apt to send the plants to leaf. Of course, on light, hungry land, it will be necessary to fork in some organic matter. In all cases work half a bucketful of damped sedge peat per square yard into the top 2 in., together with a good fish manure, meat and bone meal or hoof and horn meal, at 3 oz to the square yard.

SOWING THE SEED   Sweet corn, preferably, should not be transplanted. Sow the seed under cloches during the second week of April, or, in the north, delay until the end of April. Draw the drills 1½ in. deep, and space out the seeds at 9 in. apart in the case of Canada Cross and 12 in. apart with the taller varieties. Under large cloches sow two rows 8 in. apart. After sowing, cover the cloches, and close the ends of the rows with a sheet of glass. When the risk of frost has passed, the cloches can be removed and the sweet corn will develop well in the open.

GENERAL NOTES   Always give sweet corn full sunshine and, if possible, arrange the crop in a block rather than in one or two rows, as this gives a better chance of pollination. There is no evidence that the removal of side shoots is advantageous. In dry weather water well, or mulch with damp horticultural peat.

HARVESTING   After fertilization, the grains pass through a watery, then a milky, and finally a doughy stage. The cobs are ready for eating at the milky stage. This is usually 3½ weeks from the time that flowering commences. The 'silks' should then be withered and brown. To find when this stage is reached, part of the sheath of a cob should be pulled back and one of the grains pressed with your thumbnail. The contents should spurt out and have the consistency of clotted cream. Always use sweet corn as soon as possible after picking.

COOKING   Strip off the husks, put the cobs in boiling water for 6 minutes, drain off the water and serve hot with a knob of butter and pepper and salt to taste.

VARIETIES

Canada Cross	The earliest and best, ready the third week of July.
Early Xtra Sweet	A good early variety, must be grown on its own.
Kelvedon Glory	Early, reliable, first-class flavour.

Soya Beans

This crop is ideal for cloches, because outdoors on summer nights in England without any cloche covering may not be warm enough. The beans do best if their minimum night temperature is about 55 degrees F.

SOILS AND MANURES   As for french beans.

SITUATION   Soya beans seem to do best in a north border, for they are what is known as short-day plants and prefer a short sunny day to a full day of sun.

SOWING THE SEED   Sow the seed in exactly the same way as

french beans – the same distance apart, remembering that the plants grow 2 ft in height. To get the best results, keep the plants covered with barn-type cloches until harvesting time. It is possible, of course, to start with tent cloches until the plants grow too tall for these.

The beans can be grown in a shallow trench. This gives the cloches extra height and the young plants have more shade when they need it.

HARVESTING   The pods may be picked when young and the beans thrashed out green and used as green peas, or the pods may be left on the plants to ripen fully, when the beans may be thrashed out and used as haricot beans. In both cases the flavour is unique.

14 Fruit

Cloches are not too low for the normal cultivation of plums and peaches, and in fact cordon apples and pears have been grown under cloches when trained parallel to the soil.

The two fruits that can, however, be grown under cloches with advantage and success are strawberries and raspberries, although there should be no difficulty in growing blackberries, loganberries and similar cane fruits, provided they are specially trained along low wires.

The obvious advantages of using continuous cloches are that protection can be given against frosts, which can easily ruin a strawberry crop, for instance, and that the fruit concerned will be ready to pick from a fortnight to a month before the ordinary outdoor crops.

Strawberries

Strawberries were one of the first crops to be grown on a commercial scale under continuous cloches. The fruit ripens during the second or third week of May, according to the locality and season.

SOILS AND MANURES   Strawberries prefer a deep, free-working loam. Early strawberries do best on a light soil rather than heavy one. Different varieties prefer different soils. Royal Sovereign, for instance, likes a light soil and Red Gauntlet does well on heavier land. There are Cambridge Seedlings to suit all soils. Care should be taken to see that the soil never gets waterlogged at any time of the year.

Good powdery dark brown compost should be applied between the rows. In addition, more concentrated organic fertilizers may be given. Meat and bone meal or a good fish manure may be applied along the rows 14 days before blossoming time, at the rate of 2 oz per yard run. Early each autumn wood ashes may be given at 8 oz per square yard. If the land is particularly light, give steamed bone flour as well, at the rate of 3 oz to the square yard. This may be applied at the same time as the wood ashes.

106

About 2 weeks before planting, fork in lightly a dressing of dark brown powdery compost at the rate of, say, one good barrowload to 8 square yard, plus the wood ashes (together with the meat and bone meal). If it is not convenient to apply the top dressing just before blossoming, this may be put on about the end of February, just before covering the rows with cloches.

PLANTING   Maidens obtained from virus-free plants should always be used. Plant in mid-August preferably, or early September, rather than in October or early the following spring.

Plant with a trowel, not with a dibber, making a hole large enough to spread out the roots. The soil should be free-working and strawberries should never be put into the ground when the soil is either too wet or too dry. Firm planting is essential, and care should be taken not to bury the crown of the plant.

When planting to cover with cloches, the rows should be planned to fit in with the scheme adopted.

Method no. 1. Arrange the rows 22 in. and 42 in. apart alternately. Put the plants in 9 in. apart in the rows. With this scheme an adequate pathway is left between every two rows of cloches. Suitable for Royal Sovereigns.

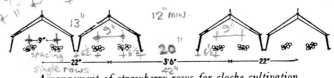

Arrangement of strawberry rows for cloche cultivation

Method no. 2. Put the plants in double rows, allowing 8 in. between the rows and 12 in. between the plants. Suitable for varieties which make little top growth. It can be used for Royal Sovereigns provided that large cloches are used.

GENERAL NOTES   If rows of strawberries can be covered with cloches from January onwards, very early crops result, for the roots are warmed and the whole plant starts to grow 6 weeks or so earlier than those outside.

If, however, the cloches are in use over some other crop – say lettuces – then these cloches should be put into position in March, and even then strawberries can be picked 2–3 weeks before those outside.

Cloches are as a rule used only to cover maiden plants. If the plants are to be kept for open air cropping for another season or two, every other plant should be taken out at the end of the first year.

INTERCROPPING   Winter lettuce can be grown as a catch-crop before the cloches are required for the strawberries. The lettuce is sown in an adjoining strip of ground in early autumn and covered with cloches in October. It will be ready to cut in November or December, before the cloches are required for the strawberries.

To ensure that the cloches are in a straight line, it is a good plan to put down a garden line first of all, and line up with that. The cloches should be touching, but an extra piece of glass should be supported at the end of each row to exclude cold air.

As soon as there is a warm spell in April, the cloches should be opened at the ridge, using the ventilating handles, and after that they should be left ventilated. Remove weeds, stir the soil lightly and apply the manure and fish manure, if this was not done in February.

A top dressing of sedge peat should be given while the blossom trusses are still erect. It is advisable at this time, too, to spray the inside of the cloches with a light whitewash flecking. This does not prevent the fruit from ripening properly, but protects it from sun-scorch.

As strawberries contain 80 per cent water, irrigation is necessary as the berries are forming. It is not necessary to remove the cloches for this purpose, but the ground between the lines of cloches should be given a very thorough soaking.

Cloches not only protect the plants from frost, but also from birds, and they prevent the rain from beating down on them. Thus beautifully clean berries are ensured, with the real outdoor flavour.

HARVESTING   Pick the berries immediately they are ripe, to give the other berries a chance to swell out. Try to pick early in the day, and during very hot weather gather twice a day. After all the berries have been picked, the cloches may be removed and the peat hoed in where it lies. The soil between the rows can then be forked lightly and all runners removed.

VARIETIES

| Cambridge Favourite | Early and heavy cropper. |
| Gorella | A very early delicious variety. |

| Royal Sovereign | Best flavour, but rather late and makes a lot of leaf growth. |
| Talisman | Late, but of good flavour and a heavy cropper. |

STRAWBERRIES UNDER ACCESS FRAMES In order to get good growth during the autumn, runners should be planted up in August; four rows to a frame with 10 in. between rows, and the plants 12–15 in. apart in the row, i.e. the 10 × 4 ft cloches hold 32–40 plants and the 4 × 4 ft type 12–16 plants. Plant very firmly with the roots spread out well. A rich organic soil is essential; this means forking in powdery dark brown compost at one large bucketful to the yard run. Keep the soil just moist all through the autumn in order to ensure good root growth.

Strawberries cultivated under Access frames

Cover the plants during February. Give plenty of ventilation during the flowering period to aid pollination. Spray the plants over with clean water each morning, as this helps the flowers to set. It is therefore worthwhile having the Access mist irrigation installed for this. Keep a careful watch for greenfly during April and May, and spray thoroughly with pyrethrum immediately it is seen. It is usually advisable to provide permanent side ventilation from the month of April onwards.

It is possible to replace two sheets of glass with wire netting panels to keep out the birds. Do not cover the same plants a second year, but plant up fresh runners each August. The plants that have been covered with cloches can be thinned out at the end of the season by removing two whole rows, and leaving two rows for outdoor fruiting.

Raspberries

With the autumn-fruiting varieties there is no difficulty in picking berries in September and early October, but gathering perfectly ripened, full-flavoured large raspberries at the beginning of June, 3 or 4 weeks earlier than outdoor ones, is most unusual. This can easily be done when using continuous cloches.

SOILS AND MANURES   Raspberries can be grown in any deep, well-drained soil. There must be sufficient organic matter present for the roots to get enough moisture during the summer, when the berries swell and ripen. Farmyard manure or other organic matter should be applied along the rows in February to act as a mulch. In the autumn, wood ashes should be applied at the rate of 8 oz to the square yard and bone meal at 2 oz to the square yard. Alternatively, use a proprietary manure which will give potash and phosphates in similar proportions.

PLANTING   It is most important to plant disease-free, healthy canes; the best time for planting is late October or early November.

Arrange the canes in rows 24 in. and 42 in. apart alternately, putting them in 1 ft apart in the rows. This ensures an adequate pathway between each double row of tall barn cloches.
Method no. 1. The newly-planted canes should be cut back to within 1 ft of the ground in February, and the rows covered immediately afterwards with tall cloches, taking care to close the ends of the rows with sheets of glass. Short side shoots soon grow out, and it is these that will bear the fruit.
Method no. 2. Run a single wire for each row of canes to be planted. Strain this 10–11 in. from the ground from stout posts at either end of the rows. Tip the canes 6 in. or so, and train them as in the drawing.

Method no. 3. Some time in October select healthy one-year-old canes grown on land rich in compost and plant them out just before the leaves fall, allowing 1 ft between the canes. Give a good mulching on either side of the row with damped horticultural peat just before the canes are cut down to within 15 in. of soil level in February. Put cloches or Access frames into position, making certain to close up the ends of the row, and keep the row covered with the glass until the raspberries have been gathered. The fruit is borne on laterals which develop from the canes after they are pruned back. Incidentally, when digging up the 'spawn' as it is called, for planting out in late October, be sure to dig up as much root as possible with the cane, and plant at the same depth in the new position.

A convenient method of training raspberries to grow under barn cloches

GENERAL NOTES   To produce early fruit of high quality under cloches, it is imperative to use one-year-old plants only.

Remove any basal suckers that may appear, as they will rob the main plants of strength.

When the flowers appear, space the cloches out ½ in. apart and spray a little whitewash outside the cloches. This prevents the fruits being sun-scorched.

Water when the fruits are swelling, as described for strawberries.

When all the fruit has been harvested, remove the continuous cloches, take up every other plant, and allow the row to produce its fruit in the normal manner next season.

VARIETIES

Malling Enterprise	Very heavy cropper.
Malling Jewel	The heaviest cropper of all.
Malling Promise	Huge berries with excellent flavour.

Loganberries and blackberries

Loganberries and blackberries can be trained along low wires and covered with continuous cloches. This brings the fruit into season 3 weeks to a month earlier. It is generally thought that less is gained by using cloches with these two crops than with strawberries and raspberries.

Melons
Melons have usually been regarded as rather a difficult crop, but under Access frames they have given excellent results. They need care, of course, but then all crops do, and for the best results it is probably necessary to raise the plants in the greenhouse in pots, so that they are ready to put out at the end of May under barn cloches.

SOILS AND MANURES   Prepare the ground by digging holes 12 in. square at stations 3 ft apart. Fill these holes with well-rotted old manure or properly composted vegetable refuse; tread down well, and then cover with 2 in. of good soil. Over the top of the hole make a mound 4 in. high and 9 in. in diameter, with soil mixed with damped sedge peat at approximately 2 parts of soil to 1 part of peat; when mixing, stir in 1 oz of a good fish manure.

Make these mounds in a straight line (you may only need four or five of them for the average garden) and then cover the rows with barn cloches immediately after preparing, closing the ends of the cloche rows with sheets of glass. It will be necessary to finish this work by the second week of April. Leave the cloches in position for 3 weeks to raise the soil temperature.

SOWING THE SEED   Sow the seed singly in 3-in. peat or plastic pots in a greenhouse at the end of March or beginning of April. The soil mixture used should consist of 3 parts good soil, 1 part sedge peat and 1 part sand. Into each 2-gallon bucketful of this mixture, work in 1 oz of bone meal and 1 oz of powdered lime. Crock the pots well (if they are clay) and fill them with the mixture, making them moderately firm only. After sowing, give a light watering and stand the pots on the staging of the greenhouse at a temperature of about 55 degrees F. Keep them growing slowly, so that on the appearance of the fifth true leaf they can be planted out on the top of the mound. This will probably be some time in May.

STOPPING AND POLLINATION   Pinch out the growing points immediately after the fourth true leaf appears. Retain two of the resulting side shoots (laterals) and stop them in their turn immediately above the sixth leaf. The sub-laterals which then grow out of the laterals will bear the fruit, and these sub-laterals should be stopped at two leaves beyond the little melon which has begun to swell. Non-fruiting laterals should always be stopped at the second leaf.

Pollinate the female flowers at mid-day – as many of them as possible on each occasion. It is usual to allow three fruits to develop on the varieties Sweet Emerald and Bellegarde, but only two on Dutch Net, Large Rock Prescott and Tiger. When the fruits start to swell they should be placed on a piece of glass to keep them off the ground.

LIQUID FEEDING   When the first fruits are the size of a tennis ball, liquid manure should be given every 5 days until ripening starts. All watering and feeding should stop when the melons start to produce their fragrant smell.

WATERING AND VENTILATION   It is usually necessary to water three times a week during hot weather, and greatest care must be taken not to let the moisture settle round the main stems of the plants, otherwise they will rot. Planting the melons on a little mound helps prevent this. Always keep the ends of the cloche rows closed until the weather gets excessively hot, and even then, before removing these ends in the day-time (they should always be put back at night-time) fleck over the tops of the cloches with some lime-wash, to break up the sun's rays and give a little shade.

Melons ready for harvesting

HARVESTING   The melons should be cut when the fruit starts to change colour and the skin starts to soften around the eye. A further indication of readiness is the little crack that appears on the skin of the fruits round the stalk. The perfume always gets stronger as the fruit gets more fully ripe. Never leave the melon on the plant until it is quite ripe. Cut it just as it is on the turn, and ripen it indoors in a dry place. You can make a melon ripen quickly or slowly according to the temperature in the room in which it is being stored.

GENERAL NOTES   It is always possible to apply water outside the cloches by means of a hose or automatic sprinkler and, to make certain that the moisture goes underneath the cloches, there must be plenty of moisture-retaining material in the top 3 in. This is helped by digging in plenty of damp sedge peat round the melon mounds. Remember that melons are shallow rooters.

VARIETIES

Burpee Hybrid	Deep orange flesh, firm, juicy.
Dutch Net	The earliest of the cloche melons, average flavour, mid-season, heavy cropper.
No Name	A very sweet, green-fleshed, juicy, smooth melon, not a particularly heavy cropper.
Sweetheart	Small, excellent flavour, early, good for late districts.
Tiger	A lovely striped melon of good flavour but not so heavy-cropping as Dutch Net.

MELONS UNDER ACCESS FRAMES   The seed should be sown in a greenhouse at a temperature of 60 degrees F in April, and the seedlings that result should be planted out in late May. Dig out holes 10 in. square and 10 in. deep at distances 2 ft apart down the centre of the long frame. Fill these holes in with first class compost. Replace the soil to make a little mound and plant on this. Shade each plant for a week or so with a sheet of paper to assist rapid establishment. About 10 days after planting, remove all the leaves on the plants except the first four true leaves beyond the cotyledons, i.e. the seed leaves. The four laterals which result should be trained to the corners of a cloche square. These should have their growing points pinched back half an inch when they show seven leaves. Sub-laterals then appear which are stopped at five leaves. A third set of laterals will then appear which actually bear the fruits.

Give plenty of ventilation to let in insects for pollination, and, when the fruit are the size of gooseberries, thin them out to four or five of the best looking ones per plant. Pinch back the main growths at two or three leaves beyond each fruit and remove them; keep removing all other superfluous growths. Place the fruit on a small square of timber or asbestos to keep the bases of the fruits dry.

Watering should always be at soil level – keep water off the leaves and fruit as much as possible. Dont' water during the flowering period. Keep ventilation at an absolute minimum when the fruit are starting to swell in order to keep the growth at rapid pace.

Rhubarb

Most people like to eat rhubarb only. They prefer the tender, succulent, forced sticks – but they may not want the bother of digging up the 3-year-old roots and putting them in heat in the dark.

Cloches can be used to make the plants start into growth several weeks earlier than normal, provided care is taken to cover the ground with straw 6 to 8 in. deep in late December or early January. It is, of course, convenient from the cloche coverage point of view to arrange for the rows to be 2 or 2½ ft apart and to have the crowns growing at a similar distance apart in the rows.

SOILS AND MANURES   Before planting, see that the soil is well manured by shallowly digging in properly prepared compost at 1 bucketful to the square yard.

Rake meat and bone meal in at 3 oz to the square yard, plus sulphate of potash at 1 oz to the square yard – or use a complete fish fertilizer. In the autumn, a feed with bottled liquid manure can be profitably given.

LIME   There is no need to lime.

PLANTING   Buy good crowns – these are portions split off from old plants. Set these out at, say, 2 ft × 2 ft with the top of the crown or bud buried 1½ in. below soil level. Plant firmly.

TOP DRESSING   Each year cover the ground where the rhubarb is growing with a 6–8 in. depth of straw, preferably wheat straw, and leave this in position the whole of the season. The worms will pull it in gradually. The straw will also smother the bulk of the weeds.

HARVESTING   Do not pull the first year after planting. Gather one or two sticks from each plant in the second year and in the third year force the plants by covering with cloches in late December or early January.

VARIETIES

Hawke's Champagne	Good flavour, very popular variety with market gardeners.
Timperley Early	Perhaps the earliest kind there is.

Vines

Vines have been grown successfully out of doors in Britain for hundreds of years – certainly since the time of the Romans. It is important, of course, to grow the right varieties and to be prepared to control pests and diseases. Cloches bring outdoor vines into bearing in the third year instead of the fourth year.

SOIL PREPARATION   With vines it is important to strike a happy medium between excessive vigour of growth and perfect ripening of the grapes. Therefore it is not advisable to overfeed in any way. The normal shallow digging in of 1 bucketful of good compost to the square yard in the autumn before planting is good practice, plus 3 oz of bone meal, 4 oz of wood ashes and 2 oz of hoof and horn meal – all per square yard. Carbonate of lime may have to be given at 3–7 oz to the square yard, depending on the pH of the soil. It is important to cultivate the ground thoroughly before planting as, once the vines are in, the soil should never be stirred deeper than about 4 in.

PLANTING   The vines should be planted in rows 5 ft apart, with the rows about 6 ft apart. Each vine should be given a galvanized wire stake 4 ft 6 in. above soil level and, say, 1 ft into the ground. The stakes must be joined to one another by a galvanized wire which should be stretched tightly 18 in. above soil level.

MULCHING   It is not advisable to mulch in winter because it prevents the soil's radiated heat from doing its work in preventing serious damage by spring frosts, while it is important also to get the soil to give out as much warmth as possible in the summer when the grapes are ripening.

PRUNING   The best method of pruning is undoubtedly the

Guyot method. The drawings show it clearly. The actual points where the growths are pruned are marked and the growths which develop from this pruning are seen. At the end of the third year the two branches which are retained should be 5 ft long if they are to be vigorous enough to bear the following season. Note in year 4 how one shoot has been cut back to two buds and the other to eight buds. The long shoot is to be allowed to crop and the growth that has been pruned back hard will provide the necessary replacements.

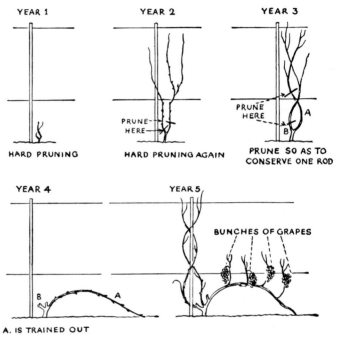

The Guyot method of pruning vines

In year 5 you see the replacements growing, tied up to the galvanized rod, and they are pruned back when they get to the top. The laterals from the other shoot are pruned at two leaves above each bunch of grapes. This summer pruning above the bunches of grapes must be done just as the bunches come into flower, for it helps the blossoms to set.

In subsequent years the whole of the old fruiting wood is cut away, one of last year's shoots is pruned back hard to within two buds of its base and the other shoot is trained out as before, being cut back to about eight or nine buds. Year after year this is repeated.

Do not expect more than seven or eight bunches of fruit per rod of vine, that is to say, anything from 6 to 10 lb weight. The rod, therefore, that is to bear this fruit should never be longer than 3 ft 6 in. and should preferably be kept to about 3 ft.

THINNING Many varieties need hardly any thinning at all, so wait a year or so before you start worrying about this operation.

TYPE OF CLOCHE It is necessary to have a tall cloche for growing vines – it is in fact the old type of narrow tomato cloche with the top glass shortened by 2 in. This allows the galvanized rods to protrude through the top of the cloche, as well as the upright summer growths when they develop. The bottom wire, of course, runs through the middle of the cloches from end to end.

Under cloches, the rod which is to bear the fruit should always be pegged to the ground as shown in the drawings. It is sometimes necessary to put a piece of glass on the ground below a bunch of grapes to prevent the fruit actually resting on the soil. The front glass must also be removed from time to time to carry out the summer pruning. This, however, is not difficult to do in the case of tall Access frames.

DISEASE CONTROL Powdery mildew and downy mildew may give trouble, and under cloches it is advisable to use a mixture of fine sulphur dust and powdered copper-lime dust. If these are puffed vigorously in at the end of the cloches to produce a cloud, the dust will travel 7 or 8 ft. Dusting may have to be done every 6 weeks in some seasons, and this is another reason why you must be able to remove the front panel. Remember, however, that as the dust travels a considerable distance, the glass will only have to be removed at, say, every fourth cloche to ensure that efficient dusting is carried out.

I find it very difficult to teach newcomers how to differentiate between powdery mildew and downy mildew and, in fact, even experts cannot do so without a microscope. A simple plan is to treat a vine with a fine sulphur dust the moment mildew is seen and if this doesn't cure the trouble within 48 hours, to use copper-lime dust instead. I hope, however, that only the mixed dusts will be necessary. Look underneath the leaves of the vine for patches of blight – you can usually tell when they occur by the somewhat curled appearance of the leaves.

VARIETIES The following varieties have proved useful when

grown under cloches. They are divided into three groups, the early, mid-season and late.

Early:

Madeleine Royale	A white, not a muscat flavour but sweet, produces a good size white berry, usually ready in August.
Pearl of Czaba	A very early white, has a muscat flavour and produces a good size berry, is claimed by some not to bear heavily enough, usually ready in August.
Sucré de Marseilles	The earliest of the black grapes, nice muscat flavour, heavy cropper, late August.

Mid-season:

Chasselas Rose	A medium-berried white grape of first-class flavour, berries tinged with red; a regular, heavy cropper.
Golden Chasselas	Very similar to Chasselas Rose but the berries are golden in colour, very highly recommended; both the Chasselases have the great virtue of hanging ripe under cloches until Christmas.

Late:

Muscat Hamburg	Large bunches, black grapes, excellent muscat flavour, ripens late September, early October, may last with cloche protection for 2 months longer, berries set rather loosely so little thinning is necessary.
White Frontignan	Produces a small-berried white grape, excellent muscat flavour, strongly recommended, can be picked about the same time as Hamburg.

SUMMER PRUNING It is possible with some large cloches to open the side panels on ventilating wires from the middle of June onwards, and if the fruiting shoot is trained forward a little, the tips of the laterals bearing the bunches may protrude through the ventilating slots. Then immediately the topping takes place, side shoots develop at the base of every leaf, and by the old method these in their turn used to be shortened. The new method is to allow the side shoots to reach a length of 3–6 in. and then to snap the side shoots off at their base rather like dis-shooting tomatoes. I call it the de-shooting method. Any new side shoots which develop outside the cloche may be shortened back in the normal way to, say, two or three buds, but as a matter of fact a certain amount of foliage outside a cloche does very little harm.

The whole advantage of this new system is that it makes the removal of the front glass something which only need be done, at the most, three times during the entire season – in fact, much less often than when growing tomatoes. An interesting point is that it is much easier to control diseases with dusts when there is less foliage inside the cloche.

Peaches

Peaches and nectarines have been grown under tall cloches for many years now. The trees are planted in a specially prepared trench 9 in. deep. This gives the cloches the extra height needed. They are planted 6 ft apart and trained on wire stretched between posts. Three wires are generally used, the first 6 in. above the normal soil level, that is to say, 1 ft 3 in. above the bottom of the stem of the peach which is in the trench. The next wire is 12 in. above normal soil level and the third wire 6 in. higher still.

The trees are trained in the fan method but there is no reason to put the big cloches into position until the trees have been in the ground for 2 years. Cloche coverage is badly needed from the middle of March until the end of May to give complete protection against frosts. If desired, the cloches can be removed in June for some other purpose and put back to protect the fruits from birds as they are ripening. Some gardeners like to keep the cloches in position all the time and so get much earlier peaches and nectarines.

The Peregrine peach does well under this system, as does Hale's Early. My favourite nectarine is Early Rivers. Be sure to remove the cloches in the winter and early spring so that the normal white oil washing can be given, using a 5 per cent solution, and be prepared to spray with colloidal copper, just as the buds are moving some time in February. This will prevent any trouble from peach leaf curl disease. The alternative is to plant three garlic corms in a circle around the base of the stem, 18 in. away.

15 Flowers

Continuous cloches are used in times of financial stress for vegetables only, but no book on cloche gardening would be complete without a chapter on flowers. Cloches and Access frames are useful in the flower garden not only for raising plants, but also for covering tender specimens or for forwarding flowers.

This chapter deals with the best ways of using continuous cloches and with the various types of flowers which have responded well to cloche treatment.

Annuals

Cloches and Access frames are admirably suited to the annual, for they ensure (1) successful germination of seed, (2) the healthy growth of the seedling and (3) natural and adequate protection.

SOILS AND MANURES   As a general rule a light loam suits annuals best. It is advisable to fork the soil 2 or 3 in. deep and apply properly composted powdery vegetable refuse at the rate of 1 large barrowload to 12 square yard.

Damp sedge peat should be raked into the top 1 in. or so.

The situation should be open and sunny, with some shelter from north and east winds.

SOWING THE SEED   Under cloches the three main times of sowing for annuals are February, March and September. September sowings are particularly satisfactory under cloches, for they give the necessary protection from cold and wet winter conditions. Those who want very early flowers can sow annuals under cloches in February, and gain 6–8 weeks. Under such conditions the cloche must be put into position a fortnight beforehand to get the soil into the right tilth.

The seed should be sown very shallowly – not more than twice its own tilth. Thin sowing is imperative. Cloches should be put into position immediately afterwards, the rows of annuals being arranged to fit in with cloche covering.

THINNING   The seedlings should be thinned to 2 in. apart as soon as they are large enough to handle, transplanting the thinnings if necessary under other cloches. The final thinning may be to 6 or 12 in. apart, depending on the height of the annual itself. After thinning, the remaining plants should be made firm in the ground.

GENERAL NOTES   The cloches may be removed early in April and used for other crops.

Sowing dates may have to vary to suit particular districts, but the dates given in the chart (see page 155) can be used as a general guide.

VARIETIES

Alyssum	A useful edging plant for dry, poor soil.
Anchusa capensis	Blue flowers, grows 18 in. high.
Calendula	Transplants well, orange flowers.
Candytuft	Excellent for autumn sowing.
Carnation	Suits light and chalky soils, sow Chabauds.
Chrysanthemum	Various annual types, needs the barn cloche.
Clarkia	Dainty pink flowers, thin to 10 –12 in.
Cornflower	White, blue and mauve, good for autumn sowing.
Eschscholtzia	Orange, red, white or yellow flowers, suits dry, sandy soils.
Gilia	Lovely blue flowers, best sown in spring.
Godetia	Pink flowers, similar to clarkia.
Gypsophila	A feathery annual for lightening effects.
Larkspur	Stock-flowered type best, thin to 12 in.
Linaria	Flowers over long period, good for light soils.
Linum	Grow the red and yellow types.
Love-in-the-mist	Blue, feathery, very attractive and one of the most popular annuals.
Love-lies-bleeding	Long, attractive, hanging, cord-like deep red flowers.
Lupin	Russell varieties are best.
Mallow	A long-flowerer.
Phacelia	Good blue edging plant, sow in spring.

Poppy	Grow both Iceland and Shirley types, raised under cloches, long-stemmed flowers obtained.
Scabious	Sow in autumn, various colours.
Statice	Sow in March, dry flowers for winter use.
Sunflower	Start under cloches only.
Sweet Sultan	Sow in autumn, various colours.
Viscaria	Sow in autumn.

Generally speaking, autumn sowings seem to be best in the second half of September and spring sowings in early March. Cloching will be necessary 10 days after sowing, or even a few days before sowing if the weather is cold. De-cloching should be done when the plants reach the glass.

As the result of sowing in the autumn and covering with cloches, flowering may be expected from mid-April onwards.

Half-hardy annuals

The following can be grown quite easily under cloches or Access frames in April, the seeds being sown where the plants are to flower. There is no transplanting, and the growth of the plants is not checked. If transplanting is necessary, it should be done in one day, and after the soil has been thoroughly moistened.

When continuous cloches are available there is never any need to raise half-hardy annuals (look for the letters HHA after the names of plants in a catalogue) in a greenhouse, as is usually advised.

VARIETIES

Ageratum	A good blue edging plant.
Aster	Sow in seed beds in rows 4 in. apart under cloches. When four leaves have developed prick out to 6 in. square. Re-cover with cloches. Plant out in beds in late May or early June.
Cosmea	Sow where to bloom, 10–12 in. apart.
Dimorphotheca	Sow where to flower. Brilliant South African annual.
Helichrysum	Sow where to flower. Thin to 8 in. Dry flowers for winter use.

Ice-plant	A creeping plant with pink or white flowers.
Kochia	Sometimes called burning bush. Sow where to grow.
Mesembryanthemum criniflorum	Sow where to flower. Thin to 12 in. apart. Likes hot, dry soils. Excellent for covering sunny banks.
Mimulus	Various coloured flowers, mostly yellows and bronzes. Likes a damp situation.
Nemesia	Sow where to flower. Blossoms orange, red, yellow, blue.
Nicotiana	Likes deep, rich soil; sow where to flower, in February, or transplant. Often called tobacco plant.
Petunia	Sow and transplant. A drought resister. Lovely range of colours in flowers.
Phlox Drummondii	Various colours. Sow where to flower.
Rhodanthe	Pink or white flowers. Everlasting. Sow where to flower.
Rudebeckia	Hates root disturbance. Flowers yellow or orange.
Salpiglossus	Excellent as cut flower. Sow where to flower.
Schizanthus	Sow where to flower. Pinch out growing point to cause plants to branch.
Ten-week stock	Sow end February, prick out under further cloches as soon as large enough to handle. Smaller seedlings give most doubles. Water well. Shade during bright sunlight until plants have picked up. When 6 in. high, late in May or early June, plant out in permanent positions.
Ursinia	Orange, South African edging plant.
Venidium	Sow mid-March, where to bloom.
Verbena	Likes light, dry soils. Sow late February and transplant.
Zea	Tall, decorative, foliage plants.

	Common name Japanese Maize.
Zinnia	Continuous cloches make all the difference to this plant. Sow mid-March. Thin seedlings to 12 in. apart.

Sweet Peas

Perhaps the annual which gives the most pleasing results under cloches and Access frames is the sweet pea. Naturally, it is important to obtain good seed from a reliable source.

The seed should be sown where the plants are to grow – say, in specially prepared trenches – during the second or third week of October. A further sowing may be made if necessary during February or early March. Draw the drills out 3 in. deep, and put the seeds in 2 in. apart. In the case of the varieties with hard coats, nick the seeds beforehand.

Cover with tent cloches immediately after sowing, or, if the weather is wet, the cloches should be put into position a fortnight before seed-sowing. When the seedlings are 4 in. high, thin them to 4 in. apart, transplanting them if necessary to other positions. If the plants are to be trained as cordons, thin to 8 in. apart. Remove the cloches the third or fourth week of March or, for extra early flowers, leave in position until the second week of April. When the plants reach the top of the cloches, the cloches must either be removed or replaced by larger ones.

Direct sowing under cloches does away with all planting out and ensures the right watering and ventilation. It ensures, too, that the seedlings grow sturdily and that the root system is never disturbed, and so the plants withstand early droughts better.

VARIETIES

Cream Ruffles	Extremely frilly flowers; longstemmed, robust.
Lavender Lace	Soft, distinctive tone of pure, true lavender.
Leamington	Pleasing tone of lilac, deep and satisfying.
Mrs R. Bolton	Deep, rich rose-pink with a white ground.
Noel Sutton	A clear, bright, solid mid-blue.
Princess Elizabeth	Salmon-pink on creamy-buff.
Sally Patricia Unwin	Golden salmon-pink on cream ground.

Signal	Very rich and bright crimson with lustrous sheen, large.
Snocap	Giant flowered, pure white.
Sun Dance	Brilliant organge-salmon with trace of cerise. Cream base.
Sunset	Bright rose-flushed salmon.

Biennials

Cloches and Access frames are ideal for biennnials, for the plants can be sown out of doors in May or June, and can then be covered with continuous cloches in the autumn to give protection, or, if preferred, very early in the spring, to encourage early flowers.

SOILS AND MANURES   As for annuals.

VARIETIES

Brompton stocks	Sow June, July, where they are going to flower, if possible. Before sowing seed be sure to give lime at 4 oz per square yard on surface. Arrange so that the rows can be covered with size of cloche used. Plant at least 12 in. square. It is possible to sow in seed bed, prick out to 4 in. apart in nursery bed, and then to transplant in September where stocks are to flower.
Forget-me-nots	Sow seed mid-May in open. In October lift plants, plant in double rows for wide barn cloches, single rows for narrow barn cloches. Plant 8 in. apart. Cover with cloches in November. Flowers will bloom late in March, early April.
Pansies	Sow seeds under cloches in March in very fine soil; adding sand to surface soil is a good plan. Plant our seedlings in shady spot, 6 in. square. Cover with cloches in November.
Polyanthus	Sow seed in February. Put cloches in position for a fortnight beforehand. Mix seed with ten times its own bulk of sand. Sow very shallowly. Prick out in shady position when three leaves have developed. Incorporate plenty of leaf mould into

ground before planting. Keep plants supplied with water during summer. Lift in October; replant close together in rows in such a way that two rows can be covered with barn cloches early in November. Continuous supply of flowers thus available throughout winter and early spring.

Sweet william   Sow seed in May. Transplant seedling 8 in. apart. Arrange plants in rows, 6 in. apart. Cover with tall barn cloches in November.

Wallflowers   Sow in open, as usual. Transplant close together. Cover with barn cloches in January. Very early flowers assured.

Perennials

Most perennials are propagated by divisions or by root cuttings. Few perennials come true from seed, but cloches can be used for raising flower seedlings just as easily as for vegetable seedlings. If the sowing is done early in the spring, the plants may flower the same year.

SOILS AND MANURES   As advised for annuals.

VARIETIES

Alstroemeria   Sow mid-March under cloches, mixing a little mustard seed in the drill. This enables weeding to be done early. Thin out seedlings when they appear to 6 in. apart. When plants are 2 years old lift every other tuber and transplant.

Aquilegia   Sow in March very shallowly under cloches. Position semi-shade. Will flower end of summer.

Auriculas   Sow in March in fine soil under cloches. Remove cloches in summer. Replace early in winter.

Border carnations   Choose light, well-drained sandy soil. Sow March under cloches.

Delphiniums   In areas where these perennials die out in ground in winter, cover individual plants with four-sided cloches. Raise

	new plants by sowing seed under cloches in February or early March. These will flower in September.
Lupins	Sow as for delphiniums.
Pansies	See biennials.
Penstemons	Sow seed in February or early March; under cloches, seedlings bloom same year.
Physalis	Sow February and March under cloches. Usually called Chinese lantern.
Thalictrum	Sow March under cloches. Transplant 8 in. apart. Transplant into border early in autumn.

Herbaceous plants that appreciate covering with cloches during winter, especially in the north, include aquilegia, delphinium, galega, gazanea, geum, lobelia cardinalis, lupins, mesembryanthemum, phlox, romneya, salvia, scabious, thermopsis and thalictrum.

Perennials that will bloom in winter under continuous cloches include Christmas roses, winter-flowering pansies and violas, sternbergias, leucojums, various polyanthus, miniature cyclamens and various anemones.

Bulbs

This section is devoted to all bulbous plants and, in fact, all plants that may be treated in the same way, whether bulbs, corms, rhizomes or tubers.

The great advantage of cloches or Access frames is that they will advance the time of flowering by a fortnight or so, and protect the blooms from frost, wind and rain. The majority of the bulbs should be planted in September, so that they can make a strong root-system.

DEPTH OF PLANTING   The actual depth of planting varies with the size of bulb. The general rule is that it should be buried its own depth. Make certain that the base of the bulb rests firmly on soil.

DISTANCE APART   Tulips may be planted in rows 4 in. apart, the bulbs 3 in. apart in the row. Hyacinths, however, which spread more, need 4 × 4 in.

All bulbs mentioned below should be planted in the autumn except where expressly stated.

VARIETIES

Aconites	Cover with tent cloches in December.
Chionodoxas	Cover with tent cloches in January.
Crocuses	Cover with tent cloches as soon as buds appear. Close ends of rows with sheets of glass.
Daffodils	Cover with tomato 'T' cloches in January. Close ends of rows with sheets of glass.
Hyacinths	Plant early October. Cover with cloches in November. When flowering spike develops, lift if necessary and transplant in bowls.

Dutch irises growing under Access frames. The tops of the frames have been removed to give the plants headroom

Irises	Cover iris reticulata, histrio and histrioides in January. Cover iris stylosa (i. unguicularis) in November.
Lilies of the valley	Cover with barn cloches in November. Result, long stems, and flowers 3 weeks earlier than those uncovered. Plant in November, firmly. Bury tips of buds 1 in. below soil.
Muscari	Cover with continuous cloches in November. Often called grape hyacinths.

| Scillas | Cover with continuous cloches in January. |
| Tulips | Cover with tall barn cloches in November. Close ends of rows. |

Anemones

SOILS AND MANURES   As for annuals.

SOWING THE SEED   Sow beginning of February to end of March, in drills 1 in. deep, 1 ft apart. Mix seed with sand to facilitate even and thin sowing. Cover with cloches immediately. Remove cloches in April. Thin seedlings to 6 in. apart. Keep bed well hoed.

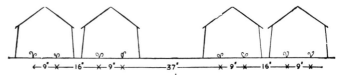

Spacing rows of anemones under barn cloches

PLANTING TUBERS   For providing winter flowers, plant in June and July. Drills 1½ in. deep, tubers 4 in. apart. Convenient to arrange double rows 9 in. apart, spaced alternately 16 in. and 37 in. This allows a 2-ft pathway between each double row of cloches.

Dahlias

These may easily be raised from seed under cloches, particularly the dwarf Coltness Gem types. Sow seed ½ in. deep and 1 in. apart in March. Cover with tent cloches. Thin seedlings to 9 in. apart. Transplant thinnings to 6 in. apart under other cloches. Keep cloche coverings until early June.

Sowings may be done where plants are to bloom, or seedlings may be transplanted.

Four-sided continuous cloches may also be used for covering dahlias planted early or for covering tubers planted in the border at the end of March or beginning of April.

Daffodils

Plant four rows at 4 in. apart and just cover them with a barn-type cloche. Leave a space of 6 in. and have another four rows; the barn cloche lines will be running parallel to one another with the bases of the cloche lines 2 in. apart. Then leave a space

of 2 ft and have your next double row of cloches with the
daffodils planted under them – as a result you will have plenty of
room to pick them.

The ground on which the bulbs are to be planted should be
prepared as described in Chapter 2 and compost added at the
same time. Firm the soil well afterwards, then plant the bulbs
about 6 in. deep, making a hole with a trowel. Some people
sprinkle silver sand into the bottom of the hole so that the base of
the bulb rests on this. Cover the rows with cloches in January.
Raise the cloches on adaptors early in March.

VARIETIES   A large number of varieties can be used but the
following have been found to do particularly well under cloches
and are therefore recommended:

Bath's Flame	Follows Golden Harvest and is similar in colour but has longer petals on the whole.
Fortune	A huge type of Helios, very popular, but bulbs rather expensive.
Golden Harvest	Golden yellow, large flowers, early.
King Alfred	A large, golden-yellow trumpet.
Rembrandt	Large deep yellow trumpet, paler perianth.

Tulips

The ground is prepared in the same way as for daffodils, and the
bulbs are planted in a similar manner. The best-sized bulbs for
cloches are 10 cm and upwards. Grow the Darwins and Cottage
tulips and not the ordinary Earlies.

Planting should be done in September, and cloching in
November. Raise the cloches on adaptors in late March, and the
cloches will be available to pass on to gladioli about mid-April.
Lift the bulbs in July and separate them, dry them off carefully
and if there are any really good plump ones, plant them in
September. Some people, by doing their tulips well, manage to
save a fairly larger percentage of bulbs each year, but for the
best results you should buy new bulbs each season. It helps if
liquid manure is used just when the flower buds start appearing
in the spring, at the rate of 1 gallon to the yard run; give a second
feed 10 days later. This not only helps to give larger and better
flowers but it also ensures a better crop of bulbs for the next
season.

The main trouble with tulips is a disease known as tulip fire
and the best control is to dust with a fine copper-lime dust. This

can easily be done by removing one cloche in eight and puffing the dust down the rows with a dust gun.

VARIETIES

Darwin tulips:

City of Haarlem	Immense vermilion scarlet flowers, best red Darwin. Height 30 in.
Clara Butt	Grows to a height of 26 in. with flowers of a delicate salmon-rose with blush tinge on outer petals.
Farncombe Sanders	Rich fiery rose-scarlet flowers with clear white base. Height 30 in.
Le Notre	Beautiful clear pink with strong stem. Height 26 in.
Pride of Haarlem	The interior of the flower is salmon-scarlet with a blue base; outside glossy carmine; early. Height 29 in.
William Pitt	Shaded carmine. Height 26 in.

Cottage tulips:

Adorno	Salmon orange, edged bright yellow. Height 20 in.
Halcro	Carmine red with yellow base; very striking, large flower. Height 22 in.
Inglescombe Pink	Bright pink shading to buff and salmon. Conical-shaped flower. Height 23 in.
Inglescombe Scarlet	Brilliant red, very large flower. Height 20 in.
Inglescombe Yellow	Glossy canary yellow; large pointed flower.
Ossi Oswalda	White changing to soft rose; large globular flower.

Gladioli

Gladioli corms are easy to grow, but they are moisture-loving plants and therefore it is important to fork in, 3 in. deep, well-rotted compost at a bucketful to the square yard and then to rake into the top 2 in. sedge peat at half a bucketful to the square yard. Because the corms are going to be covered with cloches they may be planted right at the beginning of March – this means putting the cloches into position over the ground to warm it a fortnight beforehand.

Draw out drills 3–4 in. deep, and plant the corms 3 in. apart

in the rows with the rows 4 in. apart, as for daffodils – you will
then get four rows under the large barn cloche. Many growers
plant a second batch of corms at the beginning of July to get
some gladioli in flower early in October – this second planting
need not be covered with cloches unless the weather is very wet
at planting time.

The cloches should be raised on their adaptors at the end of
the first week of May and it should be possible to de-cloche
altogether by, say, the third week of May, when the cloches can
be used for zinnias, if required. It is usually necessary to support
the spikes when they appear and this can either be done with
individual bamboos or, better still, with strings stretched tightly
along the whole length of the row, one string at 18 in., the next at
2 ft 6 in. and maybe another at 3 ft or 3 ft 6 in. The corms are
lifted with their dead foliage in October and are usually hung
upside down in a shed; about 6 weeks later it is easy to separate
the corms from the dead stems and store them in a frostproof
place for the winter.

A certain bacteria, which makes the leaves look as if they have
been attacked by leaf miner, may cause trouble. Treat the corms
in a solution of Calomel for 10 minutes before storing – dissolve
1 oz of Calomel in 1 gallon of water. Spraying with colloidal
copper works if applied when the trouble is first seen in the
summer.

VARIETIES

Alban Berg	Salmon pink, red feather.
Assam	Purple madder in centre, dark purple.
Blue Champion	Methyl purple.
De La Croix	Clear pink – red mark on clear yellow.
Mac Duff	Madder-purple, blue marking.
Mascagni	Scarlet red.
Purple Veil	Clear purple, scarlet blotch on the florets.
Rodin	Light vermilion with soft yellow throat.
Traderhorn	Scarlet-red, creamy-white feathered blotches.
Victor Borge	Pale vermilion-red with narrow white stripe.

Chrysanthemums

The best chrysanthemums I ever saw were those grown after
lightly forking in by hand 75 tons of old rotten dung to the acre.
This is the kind of liberal treatment that chrysanthemums like.

Incorporate as much fully rotted compost as you can into the soil 2 or 3 in. down, and then just leave the ground rough. In the spring, rake the land down level, apply a good fish manure at 3–4 oz to the square yard, or hoof and horn meal at a similar rate, plus finely divided wood ashes at 5 oz to the square yard.

The cloches are then put into position over the ground that is to be planted up, in order to warm it. Chrysanthemums which have been raised in the greenhouse can be planted with safety about the beginning of April, with one plant in the middle of each cloche, so that you get one long single line with the plants themselves about 18 in. apart. On light soils plant chrysanthemums in trenches 6 in. deep like celery; then when the cloches go into position, the plant is given extra head room. This can be done on almost any soil where the drainage is perfect.

Stopping is done when the plants are about 5 in. tall, usually late in April or early in May. Some people manage to stop earlier than this so that by the middle of May they can stop a second time. Stopping consists of pinching out the growing points to cause the buds in the axils of the leaves to break out and so form a much bushier type of plant. Another advantage of stopping is that it causes the plants to flower earlier.

By the end of May or the beginning of June the cloches can be removed. The plants will have grown tall and will look very healthy. From that time onwards the chrysanthemums will grow in the open.

Dwarf autumn-flowering varieties can be grown under tall

Chrysanthemums under Access frames

cloches; the plants are put out in the normal way about the beginning of May in the south and towards the end of May in the north, and then protected with cloches at the end of September or the beginning of October. This is a scheme which is more successful in the south than in the north where there may be far more severe frost. Cloches will keep out 5 or 6 degrees of frost and so protect the blooms, but they can't be expected to keep out 12 degrees of frost and guarantee that the flowers are not touched.

VARIETIES Good varieties to grow out of doors with initial cloche coverage area:

David Shoesmith	Outstanding incurved large bloom of red and bronze. Excellent for exhibition or cutting. 4½ ft.
Fire Queen	Striking colour combination – bright crimson scarlet with gold reverse. Broad, hard petals. 2½ ft.
Garden Choice	Lovely salmon pink bloom carrying four to six flowers per plant. 2½ ft.
Jane Riley	Globular blooms of gleaming white – finely petalled incurved. Strong, vigorous. 4 ft.
Margaret Riley	Perfect incurved – pretty pink. 3½ ft.
Pink Sprite	Warm shade of rose pink – crisp long-petalled florets. 3½ ft.
Shirley Sensation	Very large, solid and neat. Amber bronze. Well-shaped. 4 ft.
Yellow Nugget	Canary yellow incurved flower. True globe. 4 ft.
Yvonne Arnaud	Very attractive shade of cerise. Broad, hard petalled. Weatherproof. 4½ ft.

Carnations

Cloches are very useful for (a) ensuring that outside carnations flower much earlier and (b) giving protection to the plants in wetter districts. When preparing the soil, open clay by forking in half-rotted straw or sedge peat at the rate of a bucketful to the square yard. With light soil fork in really well-rotted compost or damped sedge peat at a similar rate to ensure that the plants do not suffer from lack of moisture in the summer. Carnations like lime, so apply carbonate of lime at 6–7 oz to the square yard.

Buy good named varieties and plant them at the end of

September in the north and about the middle of October in the south. For cloche coverage it is ideal to plant 9 in. square. Cover the carnations with cloches at the end of October and leave them in position until March, making sure to close the ends of the cloche rows. If the stems have touched the top of the glass and the weather is still cold and wet, the cloches may be raised on adaptors until, say, the end of April.

Under this scheme, it should be possible to cut good carnations from the beginning of June onwards, and disbudding may be carried out to ensure large specimens. The following October the long shoots can be cut back and the plants made compact one more, and again the cloches can go into position to give the right kind of protection.

VARIETIES

Border carnations:

Admiration	Beautiful shade of pink, delicate colour, strong growth, perfect table decoration.
Bookham Grand	A clear crimson. Giant growth.
Clarinda	Fine salmon-pink. Excellent form and strong growth.
Edenside Scarlet	Brilliant deep scarlet. Fine and large.
Edenside White	Large pure white blooms. Exhibition quality.
Exquisite	Bright rose-pink. Splendid form.
Fiery Cross	Brilliant scarlet. Exhibition form.
Frances Sellars	Rich rose-pink. Wonderful stems and petals.
Mary Murray	Yellow, perfect for exhibition.

Cottage carnations:

Cottage Crimson	Old clove perfume.
Cottage Mauve	Full flower, plant of good habit.
Cottage White	Highly fragrant.
Cottage Scarlet	Rich in perfume.
Diplomat	Salmon-pink ground specked with deep salmon.

Violets

In many parts of the county excellent violets are grown under cloches and Access frames. The beds are prepared in April by forking in fully composted vegetable waste at 1 bucketful to the square yard. In addition, sedge peat is added at half a bucketful to the square yard and is raked into the top inch or so of soil.

Buy one-year-old runners from a reliable nurseryman, and get them planted in May. Always choose a runner which has been produced close to the parent plant, as this gives the best results.

It is quite a good plan to have the rows 9 in. apart and the plants 6 in. apart in the rows, then to leave a space of 18 in. and have the next two rows planted in a similar manner. As a result it is possible to cover with barn cloches when the time comes.

CULTIVATION   Hoe regularly but very shallowly. Never let weeds develop and never allow the plants to send out runners during the summer. Watch out for red spider which causes the leaves to turn yellow – try and prevent the trouble by spraying the undersides of the leaves regularly with clean water. The variety Governor Herrick is immune from red spider but is scentless. Market gardeners often put a little violet scent on the bloom, for that reason.

CLOCHE COVERAGE   Put some damped sedge peat along the rows and in between the plants to act as a mulch. Cover with cloches late in October, close the ends of the cloche rows and keep them in position until about the middle of March.

HARVESTING   Pick twice a week from the middle of September until the end of March – it helps if the cloches have a removable panel, because the picking can then be done without having to shift the whole cloche.

DISEASES AND PESTS   Violets can be attacked by a number of pests and diseases. There's a type of greenfly, for instance, which first appears in April or May; it is controlled by spraying with nicotine, using ¾ oz of nicotine to 10 gallons of water. Before planting it is a good plan to dip the young violets into a solution of nicotine plus a little detergent to make certain that all pests are killed.

Red spider has already been mentioned and it helps tremendously if the plants can be syringed regularly. Some gardeners spray with clean water using 100 pounds pressure. Liquid derris has given good control in bad cases – two sprayings are necessary at five day intervals.

Eelworms may attack violets and become a very severe pest. It is hoped that the warm water treatment will prevent them, and those who are interested may obtain further information from the Seale Hayne Agricultural College.

Comte de Brazza	The best double white.
Governor Herrick	A deep purple, with a large flower but no scent. Much liked because it is red spider-resistant.
Lloyd George	A blue with a long stem, but not quite so free flowering as Princess of Wales.
Marie Louise	A beautiful double mauve, much liked because of its good scent.
Princess of Wales	A lovely blue.
Queen Mary	A double pale mauve, liked by cloche growers because it is such a compact grower.

Zinnias

During the last three or four years zinnias have become more and more popular and they are excellent cloche flowers. They normally grow in the Middle East and they like extra warmth. The soil should be prepared as for daffodils. The seed can be sown directly under the cloches about the last week of March in the south of England and about the third week of April in the north. It is possible to get a double row of zinnias under large cloches, the rows being 1 ft apart. The plants will be thinned to 6 or 8 in. apart when they are 1 in. or so high.

By the middle of May the tall growing zinnias will have reached the top of the cloches which should now be raised on adaptors, and they will remain in position with the adaptors giving the extra height and protection until, say, the end of May when they will be removed. The dwarfer types will grow happily under normal barn cloches. The zinnias will flower about the third week of June and magnificent specimens will be produced.

Thumbelina:

Thumbelina Mixed	Include white, yellow, pink, lavender, orange and scarlet. 4 in. high.

Button:

Button Box Mixed	Mixture of cherry, gold, yellow, pink, pearl and scarlet. 10 in.
Giant Cactus Flowered	Large, fully double flowers, 2 ft.
Giant Chrysanthemum Flowered	Large flowers with graceful twisted petals, 3 ft.

Giant Double Dahlia   Resembling dahlias, flowers of perfect form, 2½ ft.

Special notes on flowers for cutting

There are a number of flowers which are excellent when grown
under cloches. The blooms can be cut, say, 3 weeks before those
growing in the open, and the cloche-covering scheme is very
popular with growers who sell a lot of flowers.

In many cases it is advisable to use the taller type of cloche or
to use a barn cloche with adaptors that will lift them up another
foot off the ground on the wires provided together with the glass
side panels. By giving extra height in this way it is possible to
keep cloches over the taller types of perennials, annuals and
bulbs much longer.

16 Convenient propagation

Cloches are ideal for use when propagating plants vegetatively. Most plants can be raised from seed, but this in many cases is too slow for the gardener. Also, in order to obtain plants which resemble their parents in every characteristic, it is necessary to use a portion of that plant and induce it to form roots. Hormone preparations are a tremendous aid to immediate and excellent root formation.

Cuttings

Cuttings may be made in the summer or autumn. The chosen cutting or shoot should be one which is not flowering, and should be sturdy and short-jointed. When evergreen conifers are used, only the tips of terminal shoots should be taken.

THE CUTTING BED   Choose a well-drained, open situation. See that it is level and incorporate plenty of silver sand. Arrange the bed so that it can be covered with two rows of cloches close together, a path and then another two rows of cloches, etc.

Cover the part over which the cloches are to be placed with a ½-in. layer of coarse, gritty sand. If the original soil is very heavy, raise the bed slightly.

PUTTING IN THE CUTTINGS   Make cuttings a few at a time, putting them in before they wilt. Arrange the rows 3 in. apart, leaving 1–3 in. between each cutting, according to size. Make the cuttings firm and ensure that their bases rest on sand. Water immediately afterwards with tepid water. Put the cloches into position, close the ends of the rows with sheets of glass held in position by wire.

If the weather is very sunny, shade the cloches with some material. Give the cuttings a light syringing with water once a day in hot weather to prevent them flagging.

CUTTINGS TO TAKE IN THE AUTUMN   Pansies, penstemons, violas, many shrubs like veronica, evergreen conifers, and such rock plants as aubrietia, arabis, phlox, dianthus, thymus, etc.

CUTTINGS TO TAKE IN THE SUMMER Gypsophila (perennial), michaelmas daisies, scabious (perennial), phlox, and such shrubs as deutzia, philadelphus, cistus, spiraea.

SPECIAL NOTES
1. With herbaceous plants, use strong, basal shoots appearing in April, May and June.
2. With shrubs, take cuttings with a heel of old wood.
3. Don't allow pansies and violas to flower during the summer. In August cut the plants hard back. Choose young, basal growths for cuttings.

Root cuttings
Many plants are best propagated by root cuttings, especially those with thick, fleshy roots.

Plants should be lifted immediately after flowering, the roots being divided into portions varying from 1½ to 3 in. long according to root thickness. The portion of the root near the top of the plant should be cut square, and the bottom end slanting.

Where the roots are pencil-thick or more, cuttings may be 3 in. long. Where the roots are slender, cuttings need be only 1 in. in length.

PUTTING THE CUTTINGS INTO POSITION Choose a sunny site and see that it is well drained. Incorporate gritty sand into the top 4–5 in. Make straight-sided trenches 1 in. deeper than the length of the cutting. Place a little sand in the bottom of the trench and put the cutting in upright. Cover so that the top is buried ½ in. deep. Water well. Cover with cloches. Close up the end of the row with sheets of glass.

Hard wood cuttings
It is possible to use cloches to accelerate the rooting of hard wood cuttings. These may be gooseberries, redcurrants, black-currants, rambler roses or a number of deciduous shrubs. The cuttings are usually prepared by making a cut with a sharp knife just below a bud at the bottom end and just above a bud at the top end. With roses and fruit bushes the cutting may be 12 in. long, and with the deciduous shrubs about 10 in. long.

As it is advisable to have the gooseberries and redcurrants on a leg – that is to say, with a good stem – all the buds should be removed with the exception of the top three, and the cuttings then inserted 6 in. deep. Blackcurrants must be encouraged to

Shrubs being propagated under Access frames

grow from the base and so no buds should be removed. With shrubs, you will have to decide whether basal growths or suckers are required or not and whether to disbud or not, depending on the type of bush required.

The cuttings will be planted 6 in. from one another in rows 6 in. apart. The soil should be fairly sandy; if it is not, take out small trenches and lay the cuttings upright in these, throwing a little sand at their base. The great advantage of using cloches in this way is that early rooting is encouraged and better bushes are produced in a shorter time.

17 Pests and diseases

One of the great advantages of cloches and Access frames is that plants grown under them are not attacked by pests and diseases in the same way as outdoor plants, especially if the ends of the cloche rows are closed with a sheet of glass.

The turnip flea beetle, the carrot fly and the onion fly are three typical pests which seldom, if ever, damage their respective crops when grown under cloches. The reason is that the pests do not reach the plants so easily, as the glass covering keeps them away. Under cloches or Access frames, in fact, many crops are harvested before the eggs of insect pests are laid. Also, if a pest should attack, it can proceed with its work in only two directions, instead of many.

Naturally the soil pests, such as slugs, wireworms, leatherjackets, etc., are not affected by cloches at all (though slugs do not like the dry surface tilth which is always found under the glass cloche).

This chapter, therefore, does not deal with all the pests and diseases known to attack garden crops, but only with those that may attack crops grown under cloches.

Pests

APHIDES   Aphides – i.e. greenfly, bluefly, etc. – may attack plants under cloches, especially lettuces, peas and beans, carrots and members of the cabbage family. They are sucking insects, and usually attack the under surface of the leaves first. They multiply at an exceedingly fast rate, and must be controlled in the early stages.

Spray thoroughly with liquid derris. In the case of badly curled leaves, use a nicotine spray so that the fumes can penetrate under the curled surfaces. Formula: ¼ oz nicotine and ¼ lb soft soap to 2½ gallons water. Nicotine is a poison, and should be kept locked up when not in use. Derris is not poisonous, and is safe to use at any time.

CHAFER BEETLES   The grubs of chafer beetles are about 1½ in. long, have three pairs of legs, and are fat, white and objectionable-looking. They live in the soil and eat the roots of plants.

When found, fork in naphthalene at the rate of 1 oz to the square yard. This drives away the pests.

MILLIPEDES   Millipedes should not be confused with centipedes. (Centipedes do good. They have flattened bodies, and each segment of their bodies has only one pair of legs.) Millipedes have round bodies, the front four segments of which have one pair of legs each, while the remaining segments have two pairs of legs each.

Fork whizzed naphthalene into the soil at the rate of 1 oz to the square yard. This usually drives them away.

Alternatively, bury some large carrots 1 in. deep in the ground. Impale the carrots first on a stick, so that they may easily be removed. Millipedes burrow into these traps, and can then be collected, extracted and destroyed.

SLUGS   Slugs feed above the ground during the night and below ground at any time. Their eggs are white, translucent and glistening, and are the size of a tiny pearl. When digging, destroy any eggs found.

Cover the soil with powdery sedge peat. The slugs cannot move on this. When digging the land in autumn or winter, incorporate a mixture of finely divided copper sulphate and hydrated lime, mixed in equal parts. This should be used at the rate of 1 oz to the square yard. This mixture will kill any slug that touches it in the winter.

Diseases

BOTRYTIS   This is a fungus disease which mainly attacks lettuces; it is usually at its worst in autumn and winter when the light intensity is reduced and damp conditions prevail. The plants rot off at the base, and brown mouldy patches appear on the leaves.

It is most important never to allow seedlings to get overcrowded. Keep the leaves of the plants as dry as possible but the soil underneath them moist. Dust with fine sulphur dust directly the trouble is seen.

CLUB ROOT   Club root causes roots to swell and turn into a club-like mass. If opened they will be found to be very evil-smelling.

Put a piece of garlic, the size of a french bean, into the bottom of the hole at planting time.

LETTUCE MILDEW   There are two kinds of mildew – powdery mildew and downy mildew. Both appear on the undersides of the leaves. White fungus will be seen, and the leaves will then turn yellow and decay.

Never allow overcrowding. See that there is plenty of potash in the soil, which ensures firm leaves. These are less liable to attack.

Dust the plants with fine sulphur dust immediately the trouble is noticed.

Pests and diseases of fruits

APHIDES   These attack strawberry leaves and the flow of sap. They are carriers of virus diseases and may also cause curled leaves.

Spray with nicotine and soft soap – formula: ¼ oz nicotine and ¼ lb soft soap to 2½ gallons of water. Spray the crowns of the plants and cover the undersides of the leaves also about the second week of April, and again early in May.

Before planting 'maidens' – i.e. one-year-old plants – immerse them in warm water at exactly 110 degrees F for 20 minutes. This will kill all pests present on the young plants.

PEACH LEAF CURL   The leaves curl up and then turn pinky red in the latter stages; finally the leaves may fall to the ground and cause serious defoliation. The spores of the fungus winter in the bud scales and attack the young leaves directly they open.

Spray the trees just before the buds begin to swell towards the beginning of February with colloidal copper solution. In very severe attacks, give an autumn application after the leaves have fallen. Plant garlic cloves around the stem of the tree 2 ft away in a circle.

POWDERY MILDEW   White powdery patches appear on peach leaves, and sometimes spread to the fruits, causing them to crack.

Dust with a fine sulphur dust directly the powdery patches are seen. As an alternative, spray with a colloidal sulphur wash. Wash the ground, because the disease is always far worse when the soil is really dry.

Vegetable or salad cropping under dutch lights

Crop	Covered by	Period covered	Sowing	Planting	Recommended variety	Time of harvesting
Frame No. 1 (position A)						
Lettuce	1 Dutch light	end Sept.–Dec.	Seeds sown in open, 6 rows 10 in. apart, and thinned to 10 in. in the rows.	If planted out from seed bed then 10 in. sq	Sea Queen	Nov.–Dec.
Carrots	2 Dutch lights	Oct.–April	Seeds broadcast thinly late Oct. or Jan.		Amsterdam Forcing	May
Radishes	1 Dutch light after lettuce cleared	Jan.–April	Seeds broadcast thinly Jan.–Feb.		French Breakfast	Feb.–April
Tomatoes, dwarf* (position B)	3 Dutch lights	April–end Sept.	Seeds sown early March in heat.	Plant out in mid-April 8 to frame	Histon Cropper	July–Sept.
Frame No. 2 (position A)						
Beams, dwarf	2 Dutch lights	end Sept.–Nov.	Seeds sown late July in 3 rows 16 in. apart. Thin to 6 in.		Masterpiece	Oct.–Nov.
Lettuce intercropped with	2½ Dutch lights	end Dec.–April	Seeds sown thinly mid-Oct. under light not occupied by beans.	Plant out Dec.–Jan. 10 in. sq	May Queen	April–May
Cauliflower (position B)	3 Dutch lights	Feb.–April	Seeds sown thinly mid-Oct. under light not occupied by beans.	Plant out Feb. 18 in. × 18 in.	All the Year	May–June
Cucumbers	2 Dutch lights	May–Sept.	Seeds sown in heat mid-March.	May, 2 plants per light	Telegraph Improved	July–Sept.
Melons	1 Dutch light	end April–Sept.	Seeds sown in heat end March.	End April, 2 plants per light	Dutch Net or Tiger	Aug.–Sept.

* An alternative to having tomatoes following directly on after the lights become available from the carrots, would be to have the lights over self-blanching celery, planted 9 in. square until the end of May, and then to have them for covering a crop of late tomatoes. Alternative crops instead of melons, cucumbers

Timetable for lettuces

	Sowing dates	Planting dates	Period cloched	Cutting time	Varieties
N. S.	Early Feb. Early Jan.	Feb., March.	10 days before sowing, until April	May and June	Plenos Klock
N. S.	Early Aug. Late Aug.	Oct.	—	Early June	Imperial Winter Winter Density
N. S.	3rd week March 1st week April	Thin out end April.	10 days before sowing until mid-May	June–July	Hilde
N. S.	— Oct.–Nov.	Under cloches Nov.–Dec. In open early March.	1 week before sowing until planted out	Mid- to end June	Klock Delta
N. S.	Early April Early March	—	—	July	Any cabbage or cos
N. S.	Mid-May Mid-May	—	—	End July, Aug.	Any cabbage or cos
N. S.	Mid-June Mid-June	—	—	End Aug., Sept.	Mildura Mildura
N. S.	Beg. to end June Beg. to end June	—	Sept.	End Sept., Oct.	Amanda Plus Miranda
N. S.	Late July Mid-Aug.	Early Sept.	Early Oct. to end Dec.	Oct. to end Dec.	Amanda Plus Deciso
N. S.	End Sept. Early Oct.	Nov., Dec., Jan., Feb.	From sowing time to March or April	March, April, May	Miranda, Klock, Vitesse

N. = North.   Dash under the heading 'Planting dates' = no planting done. The rows just thinned out.
S. = South.   Dash under the heading 'Period cloched' = cloches not used for this crop at all.

Sowing and cropping guide under cloches and frames

The chart below shows when each crop should normally be sown and when it may
be picked under ordinary climatic conditions.

Crop	Sow in south	Sow in north	Ready
Beans, broad	Mid-Jan.	Early Feb.	May
Beans, dwarf	Mid-March	Early April	June
Beans, runner	Early April	Late April	July
Beetroot	Late Feb.	End of March	June
Cabbage, spring	Mid-Oct.	Late Sept.	March
Cabbage, summer	Late Jan.	Late Feb.	May
Carrots	Mid-Jan.	Mid-Feb.	May
Lettuces	Mid-Aug.	Late July	Nov.–Dec.
Lettuces	Mid-Sept.	—	Jan.–Feb.
Lettuces	Mid-Oct.	Late Sept.	April
Marrows (plant out)	Mid-April	Early May	June
Onions	Mid-Jan.	Early Feb.	Sept.
Peas	Mid-Jan.	Mid-Feb.	May
Radish	Early Jan.	Early Feb.	March
Spinach	Early Oct.	Late Sept.	Nov.–March
Tomatoes (plant out)	Late March	Mid-April	July, Aug.
Turnips	Mid-March	Early April	May

Northern results are always interesting. Those given below are from Barnsley, Yorkshire.

Sowing or planting date under cloches	Subject	Cloches off	Cloche grown, first picking	Open grown, first picking	Advance days
March 1	Mint	March 29	March 30	April 10	11
March 29	Peas	May 5	June 19	July 10	21
March 29	Lettuce	May 17	May 17	June 12	26
March 29	French beans	June 7	June 19	July 24	35
June 7	Marrows	July 12	July 17	Aug. 7	21

Some results from barn cloches in Lancashire

Crop	Variety	Length of cloched rows in yards	Sown	Trans- planted	Cloched	De-cloched	Picking		Quantity
							First	Last	
Lettuce	May Queen	120	Oct. 9	Feb. 5	Feb. 5	April 27	April 27	May 5	86 doz
,,	Clucas Winter Crop	120	Oct. 9	Feb. 5	Feb. 5	April 27	April 27	May 9	79 doz
Peas	Meteor	240	Feb. 5	—	Feb. 5	April 27	June 9	June 14	546 lb
Tomatoes	Stonor's Dwarf Gem	100	March 13	May 1	May 1	June 6	July 24	Sept. 7	450 lb
,,	Potentate	85	March 13	May 1	May 1	June 6	Aug. 16	Sept. 7	365 lb
,,	Clucas 99	35	March 13	May 1	May 1	June 6	Aug. 18	Sept. 15	110 lb
,,	Stonor's Outdoor	35	March 13	May 1	May 1	June 6	Aug. 7	Sept. 7	150 lb
Cucumber	Hampshire Giant	110	May 9	June 7	June 7	July 18	Aug. 4	Sept. 13	1093 lb
,,	Wither's Prize Ridge	140	May 9	June 7	June 7	July 18	July 20	Sept. 20	1548 lb
Lettuce	Unrivalled	240	Aug. 20	Oct. 8	Oct. 8	—	Nov. 23	Dec. 5	136 doz

Incidentally, the ground occupied was 750 sq. yds and the return was over £2500 per acre at 1975 prices.

Sowing and growing vegetables under cloches or frames

Note: the earliest times of sowing are in roman type and the latest times in *italics*.

Vegetable	South	Midlands	Scotland	Type of cloche (all Access frames are suitable)
Beans, broad	Mid-Jan. *End March*	End Jan. *Beg. April*	Beg. Feb. *Mid-April*	Any tall cloche
Beans, dwarf	Mid-March *End April*	End March *Beg. May*	Beg. April *End May*	Barn
Beans, haricot	Mid-March *End April*	End March *Beg. May*	Beg. April *End May*	Barn
Beans, runner	Beg. April *Beg. May*	Mid-April *Mid-May*	End April *End May*	Barn or tall cloche
Beetroot	End Feb. *Mid-April*	Beg. March *Beg. May*	Mid-March *Mid-May*	Barn
Broccoli	Beg. March *Beg. April*	Mid-March *Mid-April*	End March *End April*	Any
Brussels sprouts	End Jan–Feb. *End March*	Mid-Feb.–March *Beg. April*	End Feb.–March *Mid-April*	Any
Cabbage, summer	End Jan. *Beg. March*	Beg. Feb. *Mid-March*	End Feb. *End March*	Barn or Tent
Cabbage, spring	Mid-Oct. *Mid-Nov.*	Beg. Oct. *Beg. Nov.*	End Sept. *Oct.*	
Carrots	Mid-Jan. *Beg. April*	End Jan. *Mid-April*	February *End April*	Barn
Capsicum	Mid-April *Mid-May*	End April *End May*	Beg. May *Beg. June*	Barn

Cauliflower, spring	Jan.–Feb. *Beg. April*	End Jan.–Feb. *Mid-April*	Feb.–March *End April*	Any
Cauliflower, autumn	End Sept.–Oct. *End Oct.*	Mid Sept.–Oct. *Mid-Oct.*	Beg. Sept. *End Sept.*	
Celeriac	Mid-Feb. *End March*	Early March *Beg. April*	End March *End April*	Any
Celery	Mid-Feb. *End March*	Early March *Beg. April*	End March *End April*	Any
Colewort	April–July *Beg. April*	Mid–April–July *Mid-April*	May–early July *End April*	Barn
Corn salad	June–mid-Sept. *Mid-Sept.*	June–beg. Sept. *Beg. Sept.*	June–end July	Barn or tent
Cress and mustard	Almost any time	Almost any time	Almost any time	Any
Cucumbers	Mid-April *Mid-May*	End April *End May*	Beg. May *Beg. June*	Barn or 'T'
Egg plants (aubergine)	Mid-April *Mid-May*	End April *End May*	Beg. April *Beg. June*	Barn or any tall cloche
Endive	June–Sept.	June–end Aug.	June–early August	Barn or tent
Kale	Late Feb.–early March *Beg. April*	Mid-March *Mid-April*	End March, April *End April*	Barn
Kohlrabi	Early March *Beg. April*	Mid-March *Mid-April*	End March *End April*	Barn
Leeks	Jan.–Feb. *Beg. April*	End Jan.–Feb. *Mid-April*	Feb.–March *End April*	Barn or tent

Lettuce, spring	Jan.–Feb. *Beg. April*	End Jan.–end Feb. *Mid-April*	Beg. March–end March *End April*	Barn or tent
Lettuce, winter	Mid-Aug., mid-Oct. *Oct.*	Beg. Aug., beg. Oct. *Oct.*	End July, end Sept. *Sept.*	
Marrows	Mid-April *Mid-May*	End April *End May*	Beg. May *Beg. June*	Any
Onions, spring Onions, harvest	Mid-Aug. *Mid-Jan.–mid.-March*	Early Aug. *End Jan.–end March*	End July *Beg. Feb.–beg. April*	Barn
Parsley	Early March *Early April* Early Aug. *Mid-Aug.*	Mid-March *Mid-April* Late July *End July*	Late March *End April* Early July *Mid-July*	Barn or tent
Parsnips	Feb. *End March*	Early March *Beg. April*	Mid-March *End April*	Barn or tent
Peas	Mid-Jan. *End April* Any month following until August	End Jan. *Beg. May*	Mid-Feb. *End May*	Barn or tall cloche
Peas, Asparagus	Early March *End April*	Mid-March *Beg. May*	Late March *End May*	Barn
Peas, sugar	Jan.–May *End April*	Beg. Feb.–May *Beg. May*	End Feb.–June *End May*	Barn or tent
Potatoes	Mid-Feb. *End April*	End Feb. *Beg. May*	Early March *End May*	Barn or tent

Radishes	Jan.–April *End March*	End Jan.–April *Beg. April*	Early Feb.–May *End April*	Any
Salsify	Early April *End April*	Mid-April *Beg. May*	End April *Mid-May*	Barn or tent
Savoys	As kale			Any
Spinach, New Zealand	April *Mid-May*	End April *End May*	May *Beg. June*	Barn or tent
Spinach, Perpetual	March–Aug. *End April*	Beg. April, Beg. Aug. *Beg. May*	End April, End July *End May*	Barn
Spinach, seakale	"	"	"	Barn or tall cloche
Spinach, winter or prickly	Oct.–Feb. *End Oct., end March*	Oct.–March *Mid-Oct. beg. April*	Sept.–April *Mid-Sept., end April*	Barn or tent
Sweet corn	End March *Beg. May*	Beg. April *Mid-May*	Mid-April *End May*	Barn or tall cloche
Tomatoes	End March	Beg. April	Mid-April	As above
Turnips	Beg. Feb. *End Aug.*	End Feb. *Beg. Aug.*	Beg. March *July*	Barn or tent

Cloche and Access frame sowings for the first four months of the year

	January and February			February and March			March and April		
	South	Midlands	North	South	Midlands	North	South	Midlands	North
Beans, broad	Mid-Jan.	Late Jan.	Early Feb.	*	*	Early Feb.	Early April	Mid-April	Late April
Beans, runner	—	—	—	—	—	—	+	Early March	Late March
Beetroot	Late Feb.	Not yet	Not yet	Late Feb.	Early March	Late March	—	—	—
Brussels sprouts	Late Jan.	Mid-Feb.	Late Feb.	*	Mid-Feb.	Late Feb.	—	—	—
Cabbage, summer	Late Jan.	Early Feb.	Late Feb.	*	Mid-Feb.	Late Feb.	—	—	—
Carrots	Mid-Jan.	Late Jan.	Mid-Feb.	*	*	Mid-Feb.	—	Early March	Late March
Cauliflowers	Mid-Jan.	Late Jan.	Early Feb.	*	*	Early Feb.	—	—	—
Celery, white	Mid-Feb.	Not yet	Not yet	Mid-Feb.	Early March	Late March	—	—	—
Cucumbers	—	—	—	—	—	—	Mid-April	Late April	Not yet
Egg plant (aubergine)	—	—	—	—	—	—	Mid-April	Late April	Not yet
French beans	—	—	—	—	—	—	—	—	—
Leeks	Early Jan.	Late Jan.	Mid-Feb.	*	*	Mid-Feb.	+	+	+
Lettuce	Mid-Jan.	Mid-Feb.	Mid-Feb.	*	Mid-Feb.	Mid-Feb.	+	+	+
Marrows	—	—	—	—	—	—	Mid-April	Late April	Not yet
Melons	—	—	—	—	*	Early Feb.	Mid-April	Late April	Not yet
Onions	Late Jan.	Late Jan.	Early Feb.	*	*	Early Feb.	—	—	—
Parsley	Late Jan.	Late Jan.	Early Feb.	*	*	Early Feb.	Early March	Mid-March	Late March
Peas	Mid-Jan.	Late Jan.	Early Feb.	*	*	Early Feb.	+	+	+
Potatoes	Mid-Feb.	Late Feb.	Not yet	Mid-Feb.	Early March	Early March	+	+	Early March
Radish	Early Jan.	Late Jan.	Early Feb.	*	*	Early Feb.	+	+	+
Spinach, prickly	Any time	Not yet	Not yet	*	March	Not yet	Early April	March	April
Sweet Corn	—	—	—	—	—	Not yet	Early April	March	April
Tomatoes	—	—	—	—	—	—	Late March	Mid-April	Late April
Turnips	—	—	—	*	*	Not yet	Mid-March	Early April	Mid-April

* Earliest sowings recommended in January, but successional cloche sowings may still be made.

† Earliest sowings recommended in January or February, but successional cloche sowings may still be made.

Flower chart

Flower	Sown		Transplanted		Cloched		De-cloched		First pick	
Aster	March	8	April 27		March	8	June	13	June	30
Calendula	Plants bought		Sept. 29		Nov.	15	March 31		March	4
Calendula	Sept.	26	—		Sept.	26	April	15	April	19
Candytuft	Sept.	28	—		Sept.	28	March 30		May	23
Cornflower	Oct.	6	—		Oct.	6	March 21		April	24
Godetia	Sept.	28	—		Sept.	28	March 21		June	8
Gypsophila	Sept.	30	—		Sept.	30	April	3	May	8
Larkspur	Sept.	28	—		Sept.	28	April	7	June	6
Linaria	Sept.	26	—		Sept.	26	March 30		March	19
Myosotis	Sept.	28	—		Sept.	28	March 31		March	19
Nigella	Sept.	30	—		Sept.	30	March 31		May	15
Polyanthus	Plants bought		Oct.	2	Dec.	15	March 31		Feb.	20
Scabious, annual	Sept.	27	—		Sept.	27	April	10	June	25
Sweet peas, cordons	Oct.	20	—		Oct.	20	March 30		May	19
Sweet sultan	Sept.	27	—		Sept.	27	April	7	April	27
Viscaria	Sept.	30	—		Sept.	30	April	3	May	10

Suggested Access frame cropping calendar

Crop	Some varieties	SOUTHERN DISTRICTS			NORTHERN DISTRICTS			No. rows	In row
		Sow (s) Plant (p)	Cover	Harvest	Sow (s) Plant (p)	Cover	Harvest		
VEGETABLES									
Aubergines	Short Tom	(p) May	May–Sept.	Aug./Sept.	(p) June	Jan.–Sept.	Aug./Sept.	2	18 in.
Beans, broad	Claudia Aquadulce	(s) Jan.	Jan.–April	May/June	(p) Jan.	Jan.–May	June	4	8 in.
Beans, dwarf	Masterpiece	(s) L. March / (s) July	March–May / Oct.–Nov.	June / Oct./Nov.	(s) L. April	April–June	July	4	6 in.
Beans, runner	Princeps, Kelvedon Wonder	(s) L. March	March–May	June	(s) L. April	April–June	July	4	8 in.
Beetroot	Any globe variety	(s) E. March	March–April	May/June	(s) L. March	March–E. May	June	8	4 in.
Cabbage, spring	Harbinger	(s) L. July	Jan.–March	March	(s) E. July	Jan.–March	March/May	2	18 in.
Carrots	Early Nantes	(s) Oct. / (s) Jan.–March	Oct.–March / Jan.–March	May / June	(s) Feb.–March	Feb.–April	June	10	2 in.
Cauliflower	All year round / Snowball	(s) End Sept. / (s) Jan.	April / April	June / June	(s) End Sept. / (s) Jan.	Sept.–April / Jan.–April	L. June / L. June	6	24 in.
Courgettes	True French	(p) April	April–May	June	(p) May	May–June	July	2	24 in.
Cucumbers	Conqueror	(p) May	May–Sept.	July/Sept.	(p) L. May	May–Sept.	July/Sept.	2	30 in.
Lettuce, autumn	Trocadero Imprd. / Cobham Green	(s) Aug.	Oct.–Dec.	Nov./Dec.	(s) July	Oct.–Dec.	Nov./Dec.	6	9 in.
Lettuce, winter	Trocadero Imprd. / May Queen	(s) Oct.	Oct.–April	March/April	(s) L. Sept.	Sept.–April	L. April	6	9 in.
Lettuce, spring	Cobham Green / May Queen	(s) Jan.–Feb.	Jan.–April	May	(s) Feb.–March	Feb.–May	May	6	9 in.
Marrow	Green Bush	(p) April	April–May	June	(p) M. May	May–June	July	2	24 in.
Onions	White Lisbon	(s) Sept.	Oct.–March	March	(s) Sept.	Sept.–April	April	10	2 in.
Peas	Kelvedon Wonder / Meteor	(s) Nov.–Jan.	Nov.–May	May	(s) Oct.–Feb.	Oct.–May	June	6	2 in.
Peppers	Vinedale	(p) L. May	May–Sept.	Aug./Sept.	(p) June	Jan.–Sept.	May	1	18 in.
Radish	French Breakfast	(s) Dec.–March	Dec.–April	April	(s) Feb.–March	Feb.–April	Nov./Dec.	10	1/4 in.
Sweet corn	Northern Cross	(s) April	April–May	July	(s) April	April–June	July	4	9 in.
Tomatoes (bush)	Amateur	(p) April	April–Sept.	Aug./Sept.	(p) May	May–Sept.	Aug./Sept.	2	24 in.
FRUIT									
Melons	Tiger, Dutch Net	(p) L. May	May–Sept.	Aug./Sept.	(p) June	June–Sept.	Aug./Sept.	1	24 in.
Raspberries	Malling Promise	(p) Nov.	Feb.–May	June				2	12 in.
Strawberries	Cam. Favourite	(p) Aug.–Sept.	Feb.–May	May	(p) Aug.–Sept.	Feb.–June	June	4	12 in.
Strawberries	Remontant type	(p) Sept.	Sept.–Oct.	Aug./Oct.	(p) Sept.	Sept.–Oct.	Aug./Oct.	2	18 in.

Index